THE UNIFYING WORD

JOHN K. WORTINGER

authorHOUSE®

AuthorHouse™
1663 Liberty Drive
Bloomington, IN 47403
www.authorhouse.com
Phone: 1 (800) 839-8640

Published by AuthorHouse   11/11/2015

ISBN: 978-1-5049-6112-7 (sc)
ISBN: 978-1-5049-6110-3 (hc)
ISBN: 978-1-5049-6111-0 (e)

Library of Congress Control Number: 2015918697

ABOUT THE BOOK

Synopsis of the "The Unifying Word"

The Word of God brings unity and empowerment to people who were created in the image of God. The Word of God is within itself unified. The Word of God, The Bible, is one book, and it speaks with one voice. All scripture is held together by Jesus Christ who is himself "The Unifying Word."

"The Unifying Word" is a book which demonstrates this truth in every chapter. "The Unifying Word" thoroughly examines 26 parallels between the Old and New Testaments. This book uses a methodology of asking questions of each passage from the point of view of its parallel as a pattern for the student of scripture. Each of the parallels is a context for its corollary part demonstrating that neither testament can be fully understood apart from its parallel in the other testament. Together the parallels give a greater depth of understanding into the scripture. The parallels give evidence that God has a purpose and a plan as He intervenes in human history. This approach to Holy Scripture was used extensively by the Apostle Paul and all of the Gospel writers.

"The Unifying Word" has been written as a study of 26 of these parallels, but the book also points to a number of additional parallels that could be explored using the methodology outlined in the book. This book is an important resource for the serious student of the Bible. The book has been designed not only for individual study, but also a guided group study with a group study guide included with each chapter. The book has been field tested with several adult bible study groups.

CONTENTS

INTRODUCTION

The thesis of this study is that the Old Testament and the New Testament interpret each other. There are numerous scriptural passages that have parallels in both the Old Testament and the New Testament which will be understood best if read and studied together. The Word of God is one! When we seek to live by its guidance, the Word of God has the power of unifying and empowering our lives.

This thesis has often been challenged. As early as 139 AD challenges came, which tried to separate the Old Testament from the New Testament. Marcion was an early challenger. He was the son of a Christian bishop from Sinope on the Black Sea. Sinope is just north of the Galatia region in the north central highlands of modern day Turkey. The Apostle Paul wrote the book of Galatians to these Christians of Galatia. From Galatians we know a couple of issues which have bearing on Marcion and his background. First, there was a Christian community established quite early in north central Anatolla (modern Turkey). It is not surprising that the Christian faith would spread to Sinope, a city of some size on the Black Sea, because early Christianity tended to thrive in city environments, particularly seaports with commerce related activity. This may be because Jewish communities were often located in such settings. We know from the practice of Paul, the proclamation of the good news of Jesus often began in a Jewish synagogue and then spread to the Gentiles.

But this practice of witness also highlights the second point we learn from the book of Galatians. There was a significant backlash to the gospel, as proclaimed by Paul, from the Jewish community and from some Jewish Christians. Paul would describe some Jewish Christians as Judaizing elements in the church who argued with Paul around two issues. First, should Gentiles become Jews before becoming Christians? Second, should the church including Gentiles keep the Jewish Law and practice including the rite of circumcision? For Paul, the insistence to keep Jewish Law and practice negated the good news of Jesus Christ. For Paul, salvation comes by faith not by works. Paul argues extensively in both Galatians and Romans about this issue (Romans 2:17 – 3:31; Galatians 6: 11-16). It is important to note here, that Paul is in harmony with the critical decision of the early church at the Council of Jerusalem. The council was faced with what to do with the Gentile believers in Antioch. Acts 15 records the argument and decision which did not require Gentiles to be circumcised or become Jews before becoming Christians. The decision was that the gospel was for Jews and Gentiles. Christianity would not become a sect within Judaism.

Marcion in 139 AD came to Rome and began to teach. He rejected the Old Testament and accepted only parts of the Gospel of Luke and the letters of Paul. Marcion taught that the God of the Old Testament was a lesser God whose work of creation had to be corrected by Jesus.

Marcion's ideas were a backlash against the Judaizing elements in the church of his day which wanted to stick with Old Testament practice and were reluctant to accept some parts of the New Testament. The background and behavior of the Gentiles were offensive to the sensibilities of these Judaizing elements in the church.

While the Apostle Paul had argued with these same Judaizing elements in the church at Rome and Galatia, Paul's approach was to go to the Old Testament to develop his argument. He specifically went to the example of Abraham and showed where the Judaizing elements of the church had gone wrong as Paul brought together both the Old Testament Scriptures and the New Testament Scriptures. Marcion's attempt to deal with the issue was to cut off the Old Testament altogether and interpret Christianity without its roots and history.

Marcion was excommunicated as heretical in 144 AD. He left Rome and continued to build a following in the East. But this was not the end of attempts to separate the Old Testament and New Testament. However, such attempts are short sighted for they cut off the roots and context of the faith for Christians. Furthermore, the opposite attempt, illustrated by the Judaizing elements, that rejects all or part of the New Testament cuts off the fulfillment and power of God's promises from the Jewish faith.

In fact, the practice and teaching of Jesus and history of the early church pointed to a blending of the witness of Old and New Testaments. As Jesus begins his ministry, he traveled to the synagogue in Nazareth on the Sabbath and read from the prophet Isaiah (61: 1-2). Then Jesus applied the scripture to himself as its fulfillment (Luke 4: 16-30). Jesus would continue to use the Old Testament as a reference point throughout his ministry.

After the resurrection Jesus joined Cleopas and his companion as they walked on the road to Emmaus. Cleopas and his companion did not recognize Jesus, but their hearts burned within them as Jesus opened up the scriptures (the Old Testament) to them and taught them. Jesus began with Moses and all the prophets. Then he explained all the truth about himself in all the scriptures. There are over three hundred Old Testament prophecies which are fulfilled in Jesus.

Ravi Zacharias in his book *Questions I Would Like to Ask God* captures the scene for us. "If one could only be face to face with Him from whom life comes, whom to know means Truth and to follow means direction, how delightful would be those moments when the most confounding questions of life are raised. We are not surprised when we read in the Gospel of Luke that the men, who walked on the Emmaus Road, though unaware that they were walking with the risen Christ, said that their hearts burned within them as He opened up the past, the present, and the future to them. When they realized who He was, a light for all history had been turned on." That scene makes it clear that there is unity of purpose in what God has been about through-out history. That unity of purpose is now focused in Jesus Christ, who is now raised from the dead and now revealed for who He is.

Jesus throughout his ministry and after the resurrection sets the pattern of placing his ministry within the context of the Old Testament. The witness of the apostles and the early church practice was to do the same thing. The early sermons of the apostles are heavily rooted in the Old Testament scriptures.

Peter delivers the first sermon of the apostles recorded in scripture on the day of Pentecost (Acts 2:14-42). Peter begins the sermon by quoting the prophet Joel. In the sermon, he connects the experience of the coming of the Holy Spirit upon the disciples with the promised out pouring of the Spirit of God which was promised by God through the prophecy of Joel. Peter then quotes

David, the great King of Israel, in the 16th Psalm as foreshadowing the resurrection of Jesus.

Jesus is the Holy One of whom David spoke, who would not see decay. The resurrection, Peter says, is not a surprise, but the fulfilment of God's plan which was of old and is now fulfilled in our presence. In proclaiming both the out pouring of the Holy Spirit and the resurrection of Jesus, Peter reminds the Israelites before him of the witness of the prophets and the great king of Israel, who had promised these very things. Then Peter delivers the heart of his proclamation, "Therefore let the entire house of Israel know with certainty that God has made him both Lord and Messiah, this Jesus whom you crucified" (Acts 2:36). Peter is clear that Jesus is the long awaited Messiah, the fulfillment of the promises of God spoken by prophets and kings and recorded in the Old Testament. Peter connects the Old Testament and what will become the New Testament as a continuation of God's work of salvation for the people he created in His own image. It is all one story which has one purpose, the redemption of humankind.

The apostle Paul reinforces this understanding of one story with one purpose when he tells King Agrippa, "I am saying nothing beyond what the prophets and Moses said would happen" (Acts 26:22). More pointedly, the Apostle Paul, in his letter to the Ephesians, makes a case for Gentiles, who were at one time strangers to the covenants of promise, becoming fellow members of the household of God with the commonwealth of Israel. Gentiles and Jews are joined together into a holy temple in the Lord "built upon the foundation of the apostles and the prophets, with Christ Jesus himself as the cornerstone" (Ephesians 2:20-22).

Not all interpreters see the reference to the prophets as referring to the Old Testament prophets. However this, I believe, is precisely the line of argument that the Apostle Paul has used in Ephesians 2: 11-22 as he pleads the case for unity in Christ. The unity he argues for is the unity of Gentiles and Jewish believers who are united together in Christ. Ephesians 2:14 puts it "Christ Jesus is our peace; in his flesh he has made both groups into one and has broken down the dividing wall." So then Paul, in referring to the foundation of this temple in the Lord, is picking up a foundational element from both groups, which is from both the apostles and the prophets. Prophets here would clearly refer to the Old Testament Prophets. The Apostles refers to the News Testament leaders of the church. This dual foundation is welded into one by the cornerstone which is Jesus Christ. Both the New Testament apostles and the Old Testament prophets proclaim Christ Jesus. Most notable among the Old Testament prophets proclaiming Christ is Isaiah.

The picture that Paul draws is the new temple brought together in Christ uniting Gentiles and Jews through his blood. The purpose of Christ according to Paul is "that he [Christ] might create in himself one new humanity in place of the two, thus making peace, and might reconcile both groups to God in one body through the Cross" (Ephesians 2:15-16).

The clear implication of Paul is that Old and New Testaments both proclaim Christ who is the cornerstone of a holy temple in the Lord. The church is built on a joint foundation of the apostles, whose testimony forms the New Testament and the prophets, whose testimony is proclaimed in the Old Testament. The two are joined by the cornerstone who is Jesus, the Christ.

Alfred Edersheim in his book, *Bible History, Old Testament* describes this sense of Christ at the center of scripture in this way: "For, properly understood, the scripture is all full of Christ, and all intended to point to Christ as our only Savior. It is not only the law, which is a schoolmaster unto Christ, nor types, which are shadows of Christ, nor yet prophecies, which are predictions of Christ; but the whole Old Testament history is full of Christ. Even where persons are not, events may be types."

After the ascension of Jesus, and the apostles and early leaders of the church gathered in the Upper Room, they spent their time in prayer and the study of scripture. When the Holy Spirit comes upon them on the day of Pentecost, Peter immediately puts the event in the context of the prophet Joel as he preaches for the first time to the crowd, as noted earlier. When Stephen makes his defense before the council in Jerusalem, he rooted his witness firmly in the Old Testament record of God's covenant beginning with Abraham and now fulfilled in Jesus (Acts 7).

As the pattern of worship began to develop in the early church, several elements were characteristic. Early Christians praised God together. They prayed together. They broke bread together, and they read the scriptures together. The scriptures they shared together were Old Testament scriptures to which they added remembered encounters with Jesus and his teachings along with letters that were circulating from the leaders of the church such as James and Paul.

Beginning first with Mark, the stories of Jesus would be gathered together to tell a coherent eyewitness style story of the good news of Jesus, the Gospel. In each of the four gospels to be written by Matthew, Mark, Luke and John, the Old Testament and particularly the prophets were the context and reference point for all that Jesus was doing at the direction of the Father, who created, called, and had been at work in his people all along. There are some 343 direct Old Testament quotations in the New Testament, but there are many times that number of allusions to the events recorded in the Old Testament that are not directly quoted.

The Word of God is one! The Word is best understood when read and studied as one, intentionally bringing the parallel passages of the Old and New Testaments together so that the full range of what God has done and is doing might be best understood. Such a reading brings unity and power to our own spirit in the process. It gives evidence that God has a purpose and plan as he intervenes in history.

The ultimate way in which God has intervened in history is through the Word. John tells us at the beginning of his gospel, "In the beginning was the Word, and the Word was with God, and the Word was God. ... All things came into being through him. ... What was come into being in him was life" (John 1:1, 3, 4). The Word was the source of life, the unifying factor of all creation. All creation was unified and good. However, in Genesis 3, we witness a problem where the unity of creation is broken by sin. At the place where that sin had been committed, even as judgment upon that sin is passed down, there is a word of promise uttered by the Father. (Genesis 3:15) That promise moves toward fulfillment as "the Word became flesh and dwelt among us, and we have seen his glory, the glory as of a Father's only Son, full of grace and truth" (John 1:14). The purpose of the Word becoming flesh is to restore creation, to restore the people created in the image of God back into fellowship with God. In that sense the New Testament confirms the Old Testament.

In short, Jesus is the Unifying Word who has become flesh to reconcile us to God and to repair that which has been broken. The promise of the Word is seen in the Old Testament and in the New Testament where we find the fulfilment of the promise as the Word becomes flesh and comes to make the Father's heart known. The Old Testament and the New Testament are pulled together and unified in Christ Jesus, the very Son of God, and the Word who was with God and was God. To all who receive him, who believe in his name, he gives power to become the children of God.

All Scripture is held together by Jesus who is the Unifying Word. To illustrate the unifying factor of the word, I submit these parallel scriptures and the methodology of asking questions of each passage from the point of view of its parallel as a pattern for the student of scripture. Following this methodology will bring more unity in our own witness to "the faith given unto us".

LESSON 1

THE PASSOVER
AND THE LAST SUPPER

Scripture

The Passover -Exodus 12: 1-14
The Last Supper - Luke 22: 7-24; Matthew 26: 17 - 30

Overview

Much of life is centered around the table and food. Considerable time is spent in gathering, preparing, eating, and cleaning up after a meal. Family life is nurtured as the family gathers together to eat and share in the morning plans for the day and in the evening sharing how the day has gone. Many holidays and family celebrations center around food, often very specific foods prepared in specific ways. Those celebrations are held annually in specific places, and the extended family often travels some distance to gather together.

In our home each of those annual celebrations has its own unique menu. Turkey will not be served at Christmas. Turkey is reserved for Thanksgiving and will be prepared the same way that mom prepared it. Unique foods and how they are prepared often identify us with a specific family. For a mother-in-law to share the family recipes with the new daughter-in-law is a big deal. It is a way of saying welcome to the family; you are one of us.

That is the context in which we ought to approach this lesson on the pivotal meal of the Old Testament and the pivotal meal of the New Testament. In both cases the meal gives identity to the faith community. A person is really not a part of either of these communities, if they have not participated in the meal that is particular to that community. Identity as a person of faith is attached to both meals. This meal helps define both communities. Each meal has a strong remembrance element. In both meal settings, we are asked to remember God's specific action on behalf of the community and the individual. In both cases that action of God revolves around the theme of deliverance. God will deliver his people from slavery and from sin. Each meal features specific foods prepared in some very specific way. The extent of specific direction is amazing in both cases, even to the extent of how the food is to be eaten and what is to be said as the meal is repeated and remembered in the future.

But the one factor that really links these two meals together as parallels is that Jesus intentionally uses the Passover meal as the setting for his Last Supper. Jesus is very specific about our understanding his Last Supper within the context of the Passover meal. That suggests we need to pay particular attention to the themes that are similar in both meals. Several themes run through both stories. There is the theme of deliverance. There is the theme of sacrifice. There is the theme of death as the penalty for sin. There are the common symbols of bread and blood and wine. There is the promise of a new beginning. There is the theme of remembrance.

The theme of deliverance in the Passover is expressed in two different images. The first is the deliverance from slavery. Four hundred years before the exodus, Joseph had been sent to Egypt as a slave. God is at work in Joseph, and through Joseph Egypt is delivered from a seven year famine. Joseph becomes second only to the Pharaoh. Joseph brings his family to Egypt to save them from the famine as well. The family that was to become Israel consisted of seventy two persons when they arrived in Egypt. After four hundred years, they have become six hundred and five thousand men over twenty not counting the women and children. They have been enslaved by the Egyptians as they grew in numbers. They are an oppressed people. There is a contradiction in their enslavement. Through Joseph, God has saved Egypt. Egypt does not turn to God but will enslave Israel, the people who worship God. Moses is sent to Pharaoh with the message to let my people go. The Passover meal will be the celebration of Israel's deliverance from slavery in the land of Egypt. They are to eat the meal with their loins girded, sandals on their feet, and staff in their hands ready to get out of Egypt.

The second image of deliverance in the Passover is deliverance from death. The angel of death passed through the land, and the first born of every family would die before the night was over except where the blood of the lamb was placed upon the doorposts and lintel of the house where the meal would be eaten. The deliverance from death would be accomplished through the sacrifice of an unblemished lamb. The people appropriate the sacrifice by intentionally placing the blood of the lamb upon the entrance of their home.

The image of deliverance in the Last Supper is expressed by Jesus as he says, "This is my blood of the covenant, which is poured out for many for the forgiveness of sin." (Matt. 26:28) The image is deliverance from sin. Since the wages of sin is death, the implication is also deliverance from death. Sin also enslaves.

To tell one lie is to set a person up to tell another. There is an element of addiction to sin. To forgive, to break the bondage of sin is to set a person free from slavery to sin. The blood of Jesus given as a sacrifice is the method of deliverance from sin. Jesus emphasizes several times that his life is not taken from him, but rather given freely. The sacrifice of Jesus is to be seen as a part of the intentionality of God acting on our behalf. That same intentionality of God is seen in his actions on behalf of Israel in Egypt. The image is of Jesus' blood that will be shed later upon the cross

The two meals interpret each other precisely at the point that God is at work to deliver the people whom he has created in his own image. He delivers Israel from slavery and death in Egypt to set them free to be a new nation that worships him and lives by his law and purpose. The image of deliverance continues in the Last Supper as Jesus gives himself as the sacrificial lamb. The blood of lamb upon the cross breaks our bondage to sin and sets us free from the death that sin brings. Freed from sin and death, we can live in relationship with God for eternity.

The second theme is sacrifice. In the Passover scripture, a lamb is the sacrifice. The lamb is to be one year old and without blemish. The lamb is to live with the family from the tenth day to the fourteenth day of the Passover month. The blood of the lamb on the doorposts will be the sign for the angel of death to pass over that house. The roasted lamb was to be eaten so it could furnish strength for the journey to the Promised Land that was to begin the next day. A lamb being sacrificed for the forgiveness of sins was a regular practice in Jewish worship at both the tabernacle and later the temple from their departure in freedom from Egypt until about 40 years after the crucifixion of Jesus upon the cross. With the destruction of the temple in 69AD, the sacrifice of animals for the forgiveness of sin stopped.

Clearly, this sacrifice is suggestive of parallels to Jesus. John the Baptist in the Gospel of John says in reference to Jesus, "Here is the Lamb of God who takes away the sin of the world" (John 1:29). Jesus uses the language of sacrifice in the Upper Room, when he says, "This cup that is poured out for you is the new covenant in my blood." The sacrificial lamb of the Passover meal was to be without blemished. Jesus in the New Testament setting was without sin, making him an efficacious [effective] sacrifice. Jesus as the Passover Lamb is slain on the orders of the temple priests in Jerusalem. Jesus has been very specific about where this encounter was to take place. It would be in Jerusalem where the temple, the place of sacrifice, was located. Shed blood is the efficacious element in the Passover ritual and sacrifices for sin in Temple worship. Jesus' blood is shed upon the cross. The cross with its upright and crossbar resemble the doorpost and lintel of a house.

Jesus speaks of the bread as his body, which was to be broken and eaten in remembrance of Jesus. More specifically, the bread is to be eaten in remembrance of Jesus' sacrifice upon the cross. By partaking of the bread, the believer is strengthened and empowered to live a new life following the commandments of God walking into newness of life.

There is the intriguing image in the Passover narrative that says Israelites are to have the lamb in their home three days before the day of sacrifice. In the first chapter of John, we are told

Jesus is the Lamb of God. John also tells us, "The Word [meaning Jesus] became flesh and lived among us, and we have seen his glory" (John 1:14). For three decades Jesus lived within Israel before beginning his ministry of three years which culminates with the sacrifice of the cross and then his resurrection on the third day.

A corollary to the image of sacrifice is the reminder that death is the penalty of sin. That judgment goes all the way back to Genesis and the garden. Sin kills. It is destructive to the person created in the image of God. For sin to be forgiven, a blood sacrifice must be made for life is in the blood. The angel of death is the judgment upon sin. Egypt has rejected God and enslaved the people who worship God. There have been nine plagues, nine opportunities to see the truth about God and let Israel go. The continual hardening of heart and the rejection of God will bring the judgment of death. There will not only be the death of the first born, but there will also be the loss of over a million slaves and the loss of their army. Egypt will pay a heavy price for their refusal to acknowledge the sovereignty of God. Jesus weeps for Jerusalem because she "does not recognize her time of visitation." Jesus sees Israel's failure will directly resulting in the destruction of Jerusalem in the future (Luke 19: 41-43). The destruction of Jerusalem will come roughly 40 years later in 69 AD.

Jesus' death upon the cross becomes the door to new life for all those who believe. (John 3:16) Those in Egypt who believed and followed the instructions of Moses, by placing the lamb blood on the doorposts of their home, are saved from the death of the first born.

The common symbols of bread and blood and wine carry meaning through both meal narratives. The bread of the Last Supper is the bread of the Passover and so was unleavened bread. It was bread for those in a hurry. Israel had to be ready to leave on a moment's notice. They were headed to the Promised Land. Strength was needed for the days ahead would be trying and faith would be required as they faced the Egyptian army on one side and the Red Sea on another. The unleavened bread would empower them for the journey. The unleavened bread would identify them as a unique community eating one kind of bread together.

Jesus calls upon his disciples to eat the bread for this was his body. The bread of the supper carries a promise of the banquet to come in the Promised Land where we shall be with Christ. On the road to Emmaus, Jesus is recognized in the breaking of the bread by the disciples. These discouraged, exhausted disciples are energized and immediately run back to Jerusalem full of energy and excitement. The liturgy of the Last Supper calls upon us "to feed on him in your hearts with faith and be thankful" (Book of Worship of the United Methodist Church). The disciples would be entering difficult days ahead. Faith would be required. The bread is one loaf reminding the community of their oneness in Christ.

As discussed earlier, Jesus is intentional in taking the red wine of the Last Supper and the Passover and using it as the image of blood that is poured out, even as the lamb's blood was poured out as a sacrifice for many that they might have life. Wine as the symbol of blood that is poured out is common to both the Passover Seder and the Last Supper.

Both stories contain the promise of a new beginning. In the Passover, there is a new calendar for Israel. The Passover will be in the first month of a new year. It would be as if in America the year would begin with July because the fourth is celebrated as Independence Day. For Israel life is to be new. They are being freed. They will begin the journey to the Promised Land. From now on, time will be measured from how long ago God freed us from slavery in Egypt.

Jesus in the Upper Room says he is establishing a new covenant in his blood. It is a new covenant in our relationship with God. Jeremiah makes the bridge in Jeremiah 31: 31-34. It is a new covenant God makes; writing this new covenant upon the heart. The new covenant is made in the willing sacrifice of the Lamb of God for the sake of his people who believe and accept the sacrifice. Time is again marked from the point where we have experienced God's forgiving power working in our lives. It is a new life. We are no longer dead to God. Time is changed from BC to AD from the moment that the Word becomes flesh.

Passover and the Last Supper are intentional parallels in which Jesus uses the framework of the Passover to fulfill the promise of the Passover. The promise of the Passover is that we might be set free in the way that matters most. Jesus sets us free from sin and the resulting penalty of death in order that we may journey to the Promised Land of life lived in the presence of the King. The Father's plan of redemption which we see in the promise with the Passover comes to fulfillment in Jesus Christ as presented in the Upper Room and then acted out upon the cross. Jesus was eager for the fulfillment of the Father's plan, and so he says he has eagerly desired to eat this meal with his disciples. In

Christian tradition the Upper Room and the Cross are on two days, Maundy Thursday and Good Friday. In the Jewish way of calculating, both events are on the same day beginning with the supper and ending with the cross. The Jewish day begins with evening and ends with the setting of the sun at 6:00 pm on our modern following day.

Both stories demonstrate the theme of remembrance. Both the Passover and the Last Supper are to be remembered as God acting on behalf of his people. Both are meals that are to be re-enacted on a regular basis. The Passover is to be celebrated on an annual basis. When Israel forgets to celebrate Passover, it suggests Israel has forgotten God and the covenant has been broken. The Passover is intended to convey identity to Israel. They are a nation only because of the action of God in their lives. The Passover ritual conveys specific reminders of God's action in their lives. A part of the Passover celebration is a remembering of God's action in the lives of the Israelites from creation through deliverance to the present. Israel is in fact the people of God, and the people of God act in a particular way because they live in relationship with God. Their relationship with God is what gives Israel life.

In the Upper Room, Jesus says, "As often as you eat the bread; eat it in remembrance of him." In the medieval Church, the supper was to be eaten at least annually by all believers. To not partake of the supper would be to break faith with God. That would suggest that there was something wrong in your relationship with God. During circuit rider days of the church in America, the supper was celebrated quarterly at best. The frequency of celebration of the supper varies according to what denominational group the believer is associated with today. It varies from daily, to weekly, to monthly, to quarterly. In all these cases, the supper is used in remembrance, and in that celebration the presence of Jesus is experienced through faith. It is not just a past being remembered, but a present experience of God acting through Jesus in our lives which reminds us that we live in relationship with God. In fact, Christ is our life.

Lesson Plan for Study

Get acquainted – Favorite holiday meal - What food must be on the menu?

I. **The Passover is the principal festival of the Jewish tradition.**

    A. Read Exodus 12: 1-14

    B. What attracts your attention in the story?

    C. What do you want to know more about in the story?

    D. What is the promise in the story?

    E. What food items are emphasized?

    F. When is this meal celebrated?

    G. How is deliverance achieved?

    H. How do we appropriate the sacrifice?

    I. Why a continuing remembrance?

    J. Who does the Passover benefit?

II. **The Last Supper is the focal repeated sacrament in most Christian traditions.**

    A. Read Luke 22: 7-20; Matt. 26: 26-30

    B. What attracts your attention in the story?

    C. What do you want to know more about in the story?

    D. What is fulfilled in the story?

    E. What food items are emphasized?

    F. When is this meal celebrated?

    G. How is deliverance achieved?

    H. How do we appropriate the sacrifice?

    I. Why a continuing remembrance?

    J. Who does the Last Supper benefit?

III. How do the 2 meals interpret each other?

    A. What did you learn about the Passover that helps you understand the Last Supper?

    B. What did you learn about the Last Supper that helps you understand the Passover?

    C. What promise of the Passover is fulfilled in the Last Supper?

    D. What do the 2 meals tell us about God's action in our lives?

    E. As you participate in one of the meals, where is your new beginning?

LESSON 2

CREATION
AND THE INCARNATION

Scripture

Creation – Genesis 1:1 - 2:4a; John 1:1 – 5
Incarnation – Luke 1:26 – 38; 2:1 – 20; John 1: 6 – 18

Overview

Where were you born? This is a question often asked when we are trying to get acquainted with someone. Where we were born relates to who we perceive ourselves to be. Those questions of where, who, and why can have bearing on our identity - on how we see ourselves.

I was born in Mishawaka, Indiana. It was where my parents settled after my father got out of the Navy at the conclusion of World War II. They had married a year before when my father was on leave. After the war, they wanted to put the past four years behind them. They moved to Mishawaka in pursuit of work and began a family together.

Yes, I was a baby boomer. I was one of those boomers born to young parents whose lives had been interrupted and delayed by four years of war. After the war, these parent's thoughts turned to establishing a family and putting the tragedy and loss of the war years behind them.

Thirty years later as my wife and I began our own family, I wanted to learn more about where I came from. So, I began to do some research into my family history. Genealogical research is a common drive among human beings. We want to know who we are and where we came from.

I discovered all the Wortinger families in America were descended from John and Mary Ann Wortinger. John was likely an immigrant to the United States from southwestern Germany in 1804 -1806 when that region of Germany was in the midst of turmoil with France under the leadership of Napoleon. John met Mary Ann in Pennsylvania where they married and started a family. John and Mary Ann were farmers, and they moved from Pennsylvania to Ohio in search of farmland. Again in 1835 John and Mary Ann moved to northern Indiana in search of cheap farmland on the Indiana frontier where they worked to clear and transform 120 acres of forest into farmland. John was 66 years old when they moved to Indiana. Why move 250 miles at his age to a new frontier where the land still needed to be cleared and a house needed to be built?

The reason was rather simple. He had four sons in their early twenties and late teens who wanted to start their own farms and families. That pioneer spirit, hard work, and family orientation has marked the Wortinger family.

While all of that is a part of my identity and says something about me, it is also illustrative of that desire we humans have to understand ourselves. We want to discover where we come from and why we are here. But those questions really cannot be answered satisfactorily unless we really go back all the way to the very beginning. In the beginning, we find the answers to our questions about who we are. Both Genesis 1:1 and John 1:1 take us back to "In the beginning". Both passages of scripture give us perspective on the questions about who we are.

The scripture deals with those questions in the book of Genesis which is all about beginnings. The book of Genesis, and in particular chapters one and two, speak to those questions of how we came to be here, who we are, and why we are here. However, even as we approach Genesis with those questions in mind, we discover that those same questions are dealt with in the New Testament scriptures related to the incarnation. I would suggest that we cannot fully answer those questions unless we look at both the creation scriptures and the incarnation scriptures side by side.

Let's begin by looking at both Old and New Testament scriptures from the point of view of the how question. How did we come to be here? Various scientific disciplines will suggest a variety of technical theories to explain how it happened. But Genesis 1:3 gets to the heart of the creation story saying, "God said, "Let there be light"; and there was light." That will be the pattern throughout Genesis one. God speaks, "Let there be" and there is that which God spoke into being. The how of creation is that God spoke, he acted, and all creation including we humans came into being. We can argue about the technique that God used. However, the reality that scripture describes is that God spoke and the universe came into being!

In John 1:14, when John is describing the nature of the incarnation, he says, "The Word became flesh and lived among us." Isn't that exactly what happened at creation as described in Genesis 1? God spoke the word, and all creation took on material form or became flesh. Piece by piece creation came into being and took on substance (flesh) as God spoke the word calling the universe into being. In the words of John 1:4, creation came to life.

Luke gives us a more detailed description of the how the incarnation took place as he tells us of the angel Gabriel visiting Mary to tell her she had found favor with God and would bear a son. Mary wanted to know how this could be. Gabriel gives a specific description: "The Holy Spirit will come upon you, and the power of the Most High will overshadow you." That is the detailed description, but what it means is that the Word became flesh and dwelt among us. The Word took on physical substance and entered into the creation that the Father through the Word had called into being.

This however, begs the question "why". Why does the Word become flesh? Why does the Word enter into his creation? These questions further beg the question of why was creation called into being in the first place?

John, in the very beginning of his gospel and again at the end of his gospel, gives the answer to why the Word became flesh. With a sense of irony John says, "He [the Word] was in the world, and the world came into being through him; yet the world did not know him" (John 1:10). There is a disconnect here! The world does not know its creator? How can that be?

Human beings were created in the image of God. God formed man by his own hand and then breathed into him the breath of life. Adam and Eve walked with God in the garden in the cool of the evening. That was how creation was set up. Sadly, it did not stay that way. Sin intruded and there is estrangement. There is a breach between God and man. A rupture of relationship also occurs between the man and the woman. The alienation spreads so that it fractures the relationship between man and the animals, and between man and the soil. John describes the result: "He [the Word] came to what was his own, and his own people did not accept him." (John 1:11) This is the estrangement that sin brings. To be disconnected from your creator is to be lost and cut off from the very source of your being.

The Word becomes flesh because there is a need. Humankind has become disconnected from their creator. They no longer recognize him.

The Word becomes flesh so that we can see him; we can behold his glory. The Word becomes flesh so that we can see grace and truth up close and personal. But beyond simply getting reacquainted with the creator, the Word comes to build bridges back to fellowship with God. John again says, "To all who received him (the Word), who believed in his name, he gave power to become children of God." (John 1: 12) What John is saying is that the creator desired to re-establish the relationship he had with those he had created in his own image. The Word became flesh in order to be the instrument of that reconciliation. Paul gives expression to this understanding of the incarnation in several of his letters (II Corinthians 5:19, Colossians 1:20). That is the "why" of the incarnation. There had been various attempts at reconciliation previously. There had been friends of God proclaiming God's love and intent - most notably Abraham.

There had been various prophets who had called the wayward, disconnected, and alienated back into relationship with a creator who still loved those created in his image.

Now the attempt at reconciliation would be very personal. The Word would personally enter into his creation. The purpose of the incarnation would be for the creator to identify with the created and experience life as the creature experienced it. More importantly, the purpose of the incarnation was to restore the image in which human kind had been created before the fall, thus reconnecting the disconnected with their creator. Humankind would be given power to once again become the children of God, born of God. Therefore, one of the titles given to Jesus was Emmanuel meaning God with us.

As we understand the purpose of the incarnation, we also discover insight into the purpose of creation. People were created in the image of God for the expressed purpose to be in relationship with the creator. God did not create in order to then move on to some other project. God created in order to be in relationship with his creation. God is a personal God. God is purposeful both in his design of creation and in his incarnation, invading his own creation. God is a community, a family within himself. The doctrine of the Holy Trinity gives expression to this. As trinity, or community, God desired to expand the family. Out of that desire, God created human beings in his own image that he might relate to humans and humans to him.

When that relationship became broken in the fall, it produced in God a desire for reunion and reconciliation because another aspect of God's nature is love and forgiveness. We acknowledge that judgment is also an aspect of God's nature. God makes value judgments when he declares his creation good. God expresses judgment, disappointment and wrath at being rejected. Despite the disappointment, God's desire is to restore his creation to the promise of connected family in which they were first created. God's love for people of his creation tempers his judgment of human beings. The incarnation is not a new thing that God is doing, but a fulfillment of what God was about in creation at the very beginning. Luke gives expression to this divine purposefulness in his narrative of the incarnation. A virgin, a baby, a stable all speak of the Word becoming flesh to enter into his creation as a part of creation to correct that which had become broken.

This understanding of the "why" of creation and the incarnation leads us directly into the question of the "who" of creation. This understanding of "why" gives us some clear insights into the very nature of God himself. God is not only creator, but He is personal, loving, forgiving, purposeful, and a community within himself. These scriptures dealing with the creation and the incarnation both speak of God in the sense of trinity. The word trinity is not used in scripture. The term is a reference to God as being three in one, meaning Father, Son, and Holy Spirit. In Genesis 1:1-2, we find reference to God as creator and also the Spirit of God sweeping over the waters. In Genesis 1:26, God says, "Let us make humankind in our image, according to our likeness." There is a clear implication of community about the very nature of God.

John 1:1-2 speaks of God as creator and distinctively and separately speaks of the Word who was with God and was God. It is through the spoken Word of God that creation comes into being. John is clearly speaking of Jesus as the Word of God as an active part of the creation process. Jesus does not come into being at the incarnation. He existed from the beginning, co-eternal with the Father and the Holy Spirit.

The testimony of John the Baptist in reference to Jesus, in John 1:29-34, also clearly speaks of Jesus as the Lamb of God and then as the Son of God. John the Baptist also speaks of seeing the Holy Spirit descending from heaven as a dove and resting upon Jesus. The Son of God will be the one who is also the Lamb of God in order to bring about the redemption that is needed by humankind to bring them back into relationship with the Father. Father, Son and Holy Spirit are understood as God. There is oneness of purpose and nature in the essence of God who is Trinity.

The Trinity is vivid in Luke's narrative of the incarnation. Gabriel comes from the Father to announce the news to Mary of an expected Son. The birth will be accomplished through the Holy Spirit who would overshadow Mary. The Son would in fact be called the Son of God, the Word made flesh.

One of the striking things for me when I was traveling in Italy and studying Christian Art, particularly ancient art up through the Renaissance, was the vivid depiction of the Trinity in all the major elements of the incarnation. God was indeed acting through Father, Son, and Holy Spirit, to bring his creation back into fellowship with himself.

While we are talking about "who", we also need to address the "who" of humankind. Humans are created in the image of God. Jesus comes in order to restore the image of God in us, to give us the power to become children of God. Jesus himself is that image of God which we can see up close and personal. When we are asked, "What does it mean to be human?" we can point to Jesus as the original blueprint. In common parlance today, when persons say, "I am only human," they are typically referring to our fallibility. The common saying is "to err is human." The reference is to our fallen state, not as we were originally designed. To talk of our fallen state is to speak of a broken humanity. To truly be human is to refer us back to the original design. To be human is really to reflect the image of God.

God desires to be in relationship with us. In that truth resides the true meaning and purpose of our lives. We are not accidents of creation. We were planned for and wanted as the very crown of creation. We have been given responsibility, and there are expectations which we are called to embrace. Human beings were created "good" in the beginning. We were not flawed in the beginning, but we were created with free will so that we might enter into relationship with God. Free will is both our blessing and curse. Through the wrong exercise of free will, sin entered into creation and distorted it. The incarnation deals with sin and its penalty. The purpose of the incarnation is to restore to us that which was lost in the fall, a relationship with our heavenly Father.

I find it compelling that the first day of creation, which is Sunday, is also the day of the Resurrection of Jesus from the grave. It is not a stretch to see the resurrection as a re-creation. Through the power of the resurrection of Jesus, our world is re-created and the brokenness which is the result of sin is healed. Whether healing takes place in our lives or not is dependent upon our response to the resurrection of Jesus. Our healing is dependent on whether or not we invite the risen Christ to live in us and heal our broken lives.

Several passages of scripture emphasize that the goal of the Christian life is for the image of Christ to be restored in us. The Apostle Paul is absolutely vehement in this image. For example: 2 Corinthians 4:10 – "The life of Christ made visible in us"; Galatians 3:27 - 4:7 – "As many of you as were baptized into Christ have clothed yourselves with Christ"; Ephesians 4:7 – 24 – "Clothe yourselves with the new self, created according to the likeness of God in true righteousness and holiness"; Colossians 3:10 – "Clothe yourselves with the new self, which is being renewed in knowledge according to the image of its creator." John also picks up this image in 1 John 3:1 – 3 – "When he is revealed, we will be like him, for we will see him as he is."

John Wesley frequently refers to the goal of the Christian life as the restoration of the image of Christ in us. Jesus Christ is the image in which we were first created. Jesus acts through the sacrifice of the cross and the power of the resurrection to restore his image in us. In Jesus' re-creation of us, he brings healing to our brokenness.

The resurrection of Jesus brings not only a fulfillment of the life and ministry of Jesus. The resurrection also brings us full circle back to the very beginning of creation. In the resurrection, the image of God, in which humans were first created, is restored as humans respond to the healing work of Christ.

Lesson Plan for Study

Get Acquainted – Where were you born?

I. **Creation – Read Genesis 1:1 – 2:4a; John 1:1 – 5**

    A. What attracts your attention in the story?

    B. What do you want to know more about in the story?

    C. What is the promise in the story?

    D. How is creation accomplished?

    E. Why is the universe created?

    F. Who – what is revealed about the nature of God?

    G. Who – what is revealed about the nature of humankind?

II. **The Incarnation – Luke 1: 26 – 38; 2:1 – 20; John 1:6 – 18**

    A. What attracts your attention in the story?

    B. What do you want to know more about in the story?

    C. What is fulfilled in the story?

    D. Who is this child?

    E. What is unique about this child?

    F. Why is Jesus born?

    G. Why is Jesus born as a baby to a virgin?

    H. Why is Jesus born in a stable?

III. **How do creation and the incarnation interpret each other?**

    A. What does the incarnation say about creation?

    B. What does creation say about the incarnation?

    C. What is promise of creation that finds fulfilment in the incarnation?

D. What do creation and the incarnation tell us about God's action in our lives?

E. What do creation and the incarnation tell us about God and people?

F. How are creation and the incarnation related?

LESSON 3

THE TOWER OF BABEL
AND THE DAY OF PENTECOST

Scripture

Tower of Babel – Genesis 11:1 – 9
The Day of Pentecost – Acts 2

Overview

In the course of our ministry, my family and I have moved from one community to another several times. Some members of the family handled that better than others. Even so, it was always a bit of a challenge for the whole family to get connected to a new congregation and develop friendships within a new community. Two factors empowered us in that process of making a transition.

One factor was our sense of family and our commitment to each other. We were a family and were there for each other. That established a base from which we could move out and connect ourselves to a new community. That truth came home to us in a profound way when we were appointed to a new church for the first time after our children had left our home for college, careers, and marriage. We discovered how much our children had helped us get connected in a new place when that connection was absent.

The second factor empowering element was our shared faith. Our faith was shared in the family because we all felt that we were on a mission together. It was also a shared faith with the new congregation with whom we were getting acquainted. That shared faith gave us much in common which made our connection much easier.

The place where I experienced the most disconnect from others was when my wife and I traveled for 6 weeks in Italy during a sabbatical to study Christian Art. It was an independent project, and we were very much on our own. We generally found persons who spoke English, but not always. There were several occasions when communication was a challenge and that would leave us feeling vulnerable and alone. Certainly it was disconcerting to have people around us talking in a language we did not understand.

These experiences give some context to these two scriptures which address the issues of both unity and the brokenness that comes from sin. The story of the Tower of Babel is light on details, but several details do catch our attention. There is a sense of unity at the beginning of the story. People spoke the same language as they migrated together with one seemingly unified purpose. They were all descendants of Noah. From the genealogy, you might suspect they are at least the fourth or fifth generation from Noah. Their purpose was to make a name for themselves. A new start had been made, and the terror of the flood was gone from their immediate memory.

This new generation would make a name for themselves by building a tower with its top in the heavens. The ancients gave the name Babylon to their city. Babylon means "Gate of God", which gives expression to their purpose to invade the realm of

God. What united them was rebellion against God in their desire to make a name for themselves. But that purpose has within it the seeds of its own destruction. When your goal is to make a name for yourself, that will sooner or later turn persons against each other because it is my name not yours that I want on top. It is a bit like the childhood game of king of the mountain. The only way for a person to get to the top is by bringing someone else down. The reality of life is that this isn't a game, but it is a tragedy we witness from generation to generation, from one war to another.

The story illustrates the problem of sin and its resulting brokenness. What we saw before the flood continued after the flood. It is the problem of putting "I" before God. It is the "I" that is in the center of sin. Sin will always result in brokenness. Brokenness comes as a result of the judgment of God, but it is inherent within the very character of sin. The brokenness in the garden separated people from God, the soil, and each other. It soon resulted in the murder of one brother by another. The brokenness which occurs at the Tower of Babel is seen in the loss of a common language and the resulting separation. With the loss of a common language, the people are scattered from each other. There will be fears of each other and misunderstandings when their common language is lost.

As I deal with hearing loss, it is easy for me to see how misunderstandings can multiply when people do not understand one another.

This issue of a common language is where the story of the Tower of Babel and the Day of Pentecost connect. When the common language of the people is one of rebellion and making a name for themselves, the result will be brokenness and a scattering upon the earth. The resulting disunity with its fears, distrust, and self-seeking has marked our broken world ever since Babel.

The Day of Pentecost provides a long sought answer to the brokenness that has marked humankind since the Tower of Babel. The feast of Pentecost was one of the three major pilgrim feast days when pilgrims would flock to Jerusalem from all over the world. The feast was held fifty days after the celebration of the Passover. It was also called the Feast of Weeks and as such was the celebration of the giving of the Torah (the law) on Mount Sinai. Passover marked when Israel gained freedom from slavery in Egypt. However, it was the giving of the law on Mount Sinai fifty days later that made Israel a nation. Pentecost, or the Feast of Weeks, is seven weeks after Passover and is also celebrated as the day of first fruits with arrival of the wheat harvest. Today in Jewish tradition, the feast is called Shavot.

For the first disciples, the fifty days from Passover to Pentecost was first marked by the death of Jesus upon the cross during the celebration of Passover. On the third day after the crucifixion, Jesus rose from the grave. For the next forty days, Jesus appears from time to time with his disciples in various size groups from one to five hundred. On the fortieth day, Jesus ascends into heaven after having given the disciples their final instructions including going back to Jerusalem and awaiting the promise of the Father, the coming of the Holy Spirit. Jesus had first promised the coming of the Holy Spirit in the Upper Room where Jesus explained that the Holy Spirit would help them to accomplish even greater things than he had. Jesus also promised that the

Holy Spirit would unite them with each other and with the Father. For the next ten days, the disciples were gathered in the Upper Room praying, studying the scriptures, and celebrating what God had done in Jesus Christ.

On the Day of Pentecost, Parthians, Medes, Elamites, and peoples from all over the world heard in their own native language the good news of what God was doing in their midst. When the common language of the people is the worship of God, then oneness and understanding are the result.

The gift of tongues was the reverse of the Tower of Babel. The gift of tongues was the fulfillment of the need that the Tower of Babel made apparent. The Tower of Babel illustrated that communication between people had broken down and people were unable to understand one another. The Tower of Babel illustrated that people worked at cross purposes with each other, with each seeking their own ends. Now, a new reality was possible. God had acted in sending forth the Holy Spirit. From heaven came a mighty wind with tongues as of fire which appeared among them. Instead of being filled with themselves and a desire to make a name for themselves, the disciples were filled with the Holy Spirit. The gift of the Holy Spirit is the ability to bridge the gap, the disconnection caused by different languages. Galileans are heard speaking in the native language of people who have come to Jerusalem from all over the world. People speaking many foreign languages had gathered to celebrate the giving of the Law on Mt. Sinai, the Ten Commandments, at the Feast of Pentecost.

The Holy Spirit is given not just to help people understand one another. The Holy Spirit is given to bring unity to the disciples.

Unlike the people who lived before the Tower of Babel this new connection will not be a unity of their own making. This unity is the work of God as they are united together in their belief in Jesus as the Son of God. The Holy Spirit will empower the oneness of the church. Those who name Jesus as Lord and Savior will be kept on the same page. The Holy Spirit will empower their worship of God. God will be the focus of their worship instead of themselves as "the seeking a name for themselves" implies. The name that will be lifted up in this new community will be the name of Jesus. They will take on a new name in place of their own. They will be named Christian.

Peter stands before a crowd from around the world who had gathered in response to the sound of many tongues being spoken at the same time. He proclaims the name and saving work of Jesus. Peter proclaims the name we should live by. The Tower of Babel offers us our own name and whatever we can make of it. The Day of Pentecost is about connecting ourselves to the name of Jesus as one of his people who take on his name. One's name is about character and authority. There is no name under heaven in which we can find salvation other than the name of Jesus.

The crowd responds, "What should we do." Peter is clear that there are three things that each person needs to do. (Acts 2:37-38.) First, they are to repent and turn away from the futile attempt to make a name for themselves. Trying to make a name for one's self only leads to brokenness and separation from God and each other. Salvation will never be found in one's self.

Second, they are to be baptized in the name of Jesus. To be baptized in the name of Jesus is to take on a new identity, a new name, the name of Christian. Peter tells them, as you are baptized in the name of Jesus, your sins are forgiven. (Luke 2:38) The past is past. The focus is now on the future with a new name and a new community of brothers and sisters.

Third, as they are baptized, they will be empowered to live this new life. They will receive the gift of the Holy Spirit. The Holy Spirit's agenda is to promote the unity of the church and point to Jesus. The Holy Spirit empowers our worship of the Father. When you gather with other Christians, there is an atmosphere which differs from when you are in a secular group. The unifying factor of faith is that missing element in the secular setting.

When we were in Italy, one Sunday, my wife and I saw that there was a United Methodist Church located in Rome. We decided to find the church and join them in worship. It turned out to be a group of Christians from the Philippines who lived in Rome. Their worship was in Spanish, but they sang praise tunes that we recognized from our own worship back home. While we did not speak Spanish any more than we spoke Italian, there was still a sense of oneness with that community of believers when one of the members came to where we sat and welcomed us to the worship service.

It makes all the difference in the world, when you come before the Gate of God, what the reason is for your coming there. If you have come to build a tower into the heavens to make a name for yourself, you will find only brokenness and a loss of unity. If you come before God to worship him, to lift up the name of Jesus, then you will be empowered by the Holy Spirit to connect with others, even with persons you have never met before. There will be an understanding that is hard to believe is possible.

The Day of Pentecost brings fulfillment to the purpose of God to call forth a family who would find their identity as the children of God united as one by the power of the Holy Spirit. As long as we wander the earth in search of opportunities to make a name for ourselves, we will be caught up in the babel that scatters us away from meaningful relationships. Meaningful relationships with God and others was the promise of our being created in the image of God in the first place.

Lesson Plan for Study

Get acquainted - What helps you feel most connected with others? Or what makes you feel most disconnected from others?

I.   The Tower of Babel is a transitional point in the unfolding of the human story in Genesis. Read – Genesis 11:1 – 9

    A. What attracts your attention in the story?

    B. What do you want to know more about in the story?

    C. What is the promise or the need in the story?

    D. What is the history of sin, as reflected in the story?

    E. Why do the people decide to build a tower?

    F. How does judgment come to pass in the story?

II. The Day of Pentecost is a transitional point that explodes the church outward? Read – Acts 2

    A. What attracts your attention in the story?

    B. What do you want to know more about in the story?

    C. Why is the Spirit poured out?

    D. Where does the Day of Pentecost unfold?

    E. Who is present in the city?

    F. To whom is the Spirit poured out?

    G. What are the images of the Spirit that the story illustrates?

    H. What is the fulfillment that answers the need of people?

    I. What is the result of the pouring out of the Spirit?

III. How do the Tower of Babel and the Day of Pentecost interpret each other?

    A. What does the Tower of Babel say about the Day of Pentecost?

    B. What does the Day of Pentecost say about the Tower of Babel?

    C. What is the need illustrated in the Tower of Babel which is answered by the Day of Pentecost?

    D. What was the focus of unity in the Tower of Babel and how does it contrast with the focus of unity on Pentecost?

    E. What do the Tower of Babel and the Day of Pentecost tell us about God's action in our lives?

LESSON 4

THE CALL OF ABRAM
AND THE CALL OF MARY

Scripture

Call of Abraham – Genesis 12:1-9; 18:13-14
Call of Mary – Luke 1:26 – 38, 55; Matt. 1:1

A Word of Explanation

Before we begin this study, a word of explanation is needed in regard to the name of Abraham. We most commonly know this towering figure of the Old Testament by his later name of Abraham. Nearly one hundred times in the Bible God is referred to as the "God of Abraham." However, when we first meet Abraham in the scripture, when he is introduced as the son of Terah, his name is Abram (Genesis 11). Abram's name will not be changed to Abraham by God until the covenant is reaffirmed once again with God when Abram is ninety nine years old, a year before the birth of his son Isaac. (Genesis 17)

In developing this lesson, I have chosen to use the name Abram and Abraham in their proper places of reference in the scripture. The name Abraham will only be used if the reference point is after reaffirmation of the covenant with God that occurs when Abraham is ninety nine years of age. Thus to talk about the call of God to him, we must use the name "Abram".

As a further note, the name Abram means "exalted father." The name Abraham means "father of a multitude" which is in keeping with the promise God had made to Abraham. The only child of Abraham and Sarah is Isaac. Isaac will have twin sons, Esau and Jacob. Jacob will be the father of twelve sons who will be identified with the twelve tribes of Israel. Please note that Abram also has a son by Sarah's servant, Hagar, whose name is Ishmael. While Ishmael is the oldest son, the son of the covenant is Isaac, whose father's name, at the time of his birth, had been changed to Abraham. Technically, Ishmael is the son of Abram. Isaac is the son of Abraham. While Abram and Abraham are the same person, the distinction in name does point to a difference in the covenant with God at each particular time.

Overview

Big decisions change our lives. Decisions, such as who we marry, or the career we embark on, or those we decide to befriend, each make dramatic impacts upon our lives. Often those decisions are more dramatic than they may, at first, seem. Perhaps the most profound question that cuts across each of those decisions is: "What is God doing in my life?" It is a question of faith that makes some basic assumptions. One of those assumptions is that God is a personal God - a God who enters into relationship with the people he created in his own image. A second assumption is that God has a plan - a purpose for his creation. A third assumption is that God invites people to be a part of his plan and purpose for the world. These assumptions require faith, and that faith makes all the difference in life.

Without faith, life is seen as capricious and the culmination of haphazard choices by ourselves and others which ultimately have no meaning. Such a view of life ultimately dissolves into the pessimistic philosophy of eat, drink, and be merry for tomorrow we die. It is persons of faith who make the difference for good in the world.

The question of faith came early in my life. I was twelve when I felt a call from God to live my life at his direction instead of my own. From that point forward, I began following a course in life that would prepare me to be useful to God's purpose for my life. My grades in school dramatically improved because I now had a direction for my life. For me, that call involved going into ministry. For others, God's direction may be education, or medicine, or construction. The key issue is not the particular call as much as it is that we enter into a relationship with a God who wants us to be a part of his plan and purpose for the world. Our decision about whether to claim such a faith, or to run from such a faith and such a relationship, will shape our lives in significant and eternal ways.

This question of faith is the context for looking at the calls of Abram and Mary. They are arguably among those who have most made a difference in our world for good. Certainly Abraham is a focal personality of the Old Testament and Mary a focal personality of the New Testament. As we look at these two persons as they respond in faith to God who calls them to be a part of his purpose, I believe we will find some enlightening similarities and contrasts. To discuss their connection, there are six questions that form the framework for this parallel of their call. First, who are Abram and Mary? Second, what is the timing of their calls?

Third, what are the commands, or call of God? Fourth, what are the promises of God? Fifth, how do Abram and Mary respond to God's call? Finally, who is the child who is the focus of the promise and the command of God? Through this whole process there are some insights into Abraham's testimony that guide us in understanding Mary's testimony. Mary's testimony also helps understand the call of Abram.

First, who are Abram and Mary? We first hear of Abram in Genesis 11 which also records the story of the Tower of Babel which reminds us that sin is still a problem upon the earth. Abram is recorded in the tenth generation after Noah, the son of Terah. Nothing is mentioned that is remarkable about Abram other than that he responds in faith when God calls him to go. With the call to go comes the promise that Abram will be blessed and become a great nation. The call comes when Abram is seventy five years old. The call comes late in life for Abram who has no children and seemingly faces a limited future.

In Luke 1, we are introduced to a virgin named Mary who is betrothed to Joseph, a descendant of King David. Mary lives in Nazareth, a small village in northern Israel, and is undoubtedly a teenager when the angel Gabriel appears before her. Gabriel calls Mary "the favored one" but no reason is given other than that she has found favor in the eyes of God. Nothing seems to mark that favor except that she responds in faith saying, "Here I am, the servant of the Lord."

The only remarkable thing about both Abram and Mary is that they respond in faith when God calls them to be a part of his purpose. Even then both of their faith responses falter at times.

Abram's sojourn in Egypt is a case in point, as well as the whole issue with Hagar and Ishmael. (Genesis 12:10; Genesis 16) You will note that Mary, Joseph, and Jesus have their own sojourn in Egypt.

Mary's attempt to call Jesus back home from his preaching tour is her case in point. (Matthew 12:46-50) Both Abram and Mary respond with faith, but clearly their faith is disjointed and an uneven response. But just as clearly, they both grow in faith over time. With that perspective, the remarkable thing about each of them is that they are the recipients of God's grace. Is that not also true of each of us? The fact which is remarkable about any of us is that we are recipients of God's grace. Mary is young and Abram is significantly older, yet both are called. There is a hint that Abram's father, Terah, could have been called earlier. Terah had left Ur of Chaldea to go to Canaan, but he stops in Haran. Terah only went half-way to the Promised Land. It is Abram that goes all the way. Both Abram and Mary are promised that they will be blessed by their positive response of faith. Abram sees himself as the friend of God. Mary sees herself as the servant of God. Both see themselves in relationship to God.

Second, what is the timing of their calls? The calling of Abram comes in the tenth generation after Noah and salvation through the ark. However, it is apparent as we witness the construction of the Tower of Babel that sin and separation from God is still a problem even among the descendants of Noah. We are not sure when the Tower of Babel happens within the time frame of these ten generations, (I have suggested earlier that it may have been in the fourth or fifth generation) but we note it is Terah that leaves Ur of Chaldea which is in the territory of Babylon, a potential site for the tower. However, what is evident is that people are still in need of salvation. God acts not only in judgment but he also acts to bring people back to him. In Abram, God is acting by taking a new approach to dealing with sin and his wayward people.

Mary is visited by the angel Gabriel in the sixth month of the pregnancy of Elizabeth. The stories of John the Baptist and Jesus are thus connected from their births. We also know that Elizabeth and Mary are related. Some have suggested Elizabeth is the older sister of Mary's mother. Elizabeth, like Sarah, was said to be barren and had her first child in her old age. Elizabeth and Mary become a contrast with Elizabeth being barren into old age and Mary is a virgin. When you look at these two women whose stories are connected, you have to conclude God is up to something. God is at work because this is not the normal course of life.

Luke places the birth of Jesus during the reign of Emperor Augustus Caesar. It is an unusual time of peace in the Roman Empire. Thirty five years after the resurrection of Jesus, Israel will be destroyed as a nation by Rome. The Roman Empire will begin to fall apart slowly over the next three hundred and thirty years. Then things will really get bad. It is a critical time to make a world-wide impact. Sin is rampant everywhere. It has been four hundred years since the last word from God by a prophet. There is a sense of spiritual bankruptcy in the world at large. The Jewish community has spread throughout much of the known world in the larger metropolitan areas as traders with their own internal identification. Travel is the safest and easiest it has been and will be for some time to come.

The timing of the call of both Abram and Mary are at critical junctures in the history of the world. If the future is to be different than where it is headed, then something needs to change.

Third, what are the commands, or call of God? The Lord calls Abram to "Go" to the land that I will show you. It is a command for Abram to make himself available to God to go where God directed. The command to "Go," carries within it the command to leave. The Lord is quite specific about what Abram is to leave behind: his country, his kindred, and his father's house. The implication is that Abram is to make a complete break from the past in order to embrace a new future. Abram will be totally reliant upon God. The commands to "Go to" and "leave behind" require faith and trust in God and God's purposes for one's life. Radical obedience will be required.

The same radical obedience is evident in the expectation of God's call to Mary through the voice of the angel Gabriel. The call to Mary is prefaced by a preliminary command, "Do not be afraid, Mary." The purpose of this command is both to put Mary at ease and to let her know that she is known personally by God. God knows her and she has nothing to fear from God. That is quite a statement in and of itself that requires significant faith to begin with.

The commands that follow are: you will conceive, you will bear a son, and you shall name him Jesus. For a virgin, who is engaged to be married, this command is to make herself available to God. It is a call to surrender herself to God's purposes. Such a call is also a call to potentially cut herself off from her family and her community; and what about Joseph? Now to be sure,

Joseph comes around and is supportive of Mary, but Mary does not know that at the beginning. Do not forget that Joseph will need a little divine intervention. The potential consequences here are quite dire for Mary. Mary's positive assent is not an easy response and will be life changing. There will be relationships and special moments that will be left behind for Mary.

Elizabeth also appears to be supportive of Mary and perhaps intervenes with Mary's family back in Nazareth who are relatives of Elizabeth. Again Mary does not know this when she responds to the angel. In either case Mary does not spend much time in Nazareth after her response. She travels to Elizabeth soon after the visit of Gabriel and stays around Jerusalem for three months until the birth of John. While Mary travels back to Nazareth, it is but for a short time, because she and Joseph will soon be traveling to Bethlehem for the census. The child will be born while she is in Bethlehem. The family will stay in Bethlehem for a period of time, but they do not come back to Nazareth for at least two or three years at a minimum. Certainly the past is left behind and a new future is embraced by Mary as she says, "Here am I, the servant of the Lord; let it be with me according to your word." That is the same kind of whole hearted reliance upon God that we saw demonstrated by Abram.

Fourth, what are the promises of God? For Mary the promises of God come both before and after the call itself. Mary is first assured that she has found favor with God, and then she is assured that the Lord is with her. Mary is not left to her own devices. She will have help from on high. Gabriel goes on to tell Mary that the child will be great and called the Son of the Most High. The Lord God will give to this child the throne of his ancestor David. He will reign forever, and of his kingdom there will be no end. This child is clearly the long awaited Messiah, the one who will show us the face of his father. Mary, like Joseph, is a descendant of King David. Most of the people in Nazareth are probably descendants of David. Everyone knew the deliverer would come from the family of David. It is clear to Mary that God has great plans at work here. She was being invited to be a part of something that would change the world. To believe these promises will require a leap of faith.

Mary is also given some evidence that she could immediately see and trust as she is told about Elizabeth. Elizabeth is the evidence that the impossible can happen when God is involved. Gabriel tells her, "Nothing is impossible with God." The vision of a mighty all powerful God that is drawn is all encompassing.

Abram also has this same vast vision drawn for him in the promises of God. "Go to the Land I will show you", implies that God is going as well. God will be with Abram as he travels. This is not a delegated assignment. Rather, it is a shared journey of companionship. God promises to make Abram a great nation. His name will be great, and he will be a blessing to others. In fact, all families of the earth will be blessed by God through Abram. It is the same kind of message that Mary receives. All the earth will be blessed through Mary and Abram.

God's eyes will be upon Abram as God promises to bless Abram and bless those who bless Abram. He will also curse those who curse Abram. That is the promise of God. He will be in Abram's corner to actively work for Abram's welfare. It is reminiscent of the promise we hear from Jeremiah the prophet to Israel in Jeremiah 29:11. "For surly I know the plans I have for you, says the Lord, plans for your welfare and not for harm, to give you a future with hope." Jeremiah speaks that prophecy while looking at the coming exile of Israel. Abram hears these promises from God knowing that he is seventy five years old with no children. His wife Sarah has been barren. To believe these promises will require a leap of faith.

Fifth, how do Abram and Mary respond to God's call? The scripture does not suggest any hesitancy in Abram. The scripture simply says, "So Abram went." Abram packed up his family and his flocks and headed west. As Abram comes into the Promised Land, the Lord appears to Abram and affirms the promise of giving the land to Abram's offspring. Even though Abram is still childless, his response is to build an altar to the Lord. The child of promise will not be born for another twenty five years. Nevertheless, Abram builds a new altar as he moves to each new place and invokes the name of the Lord over the next twenty five years. The response of Abram was first obedience; then he worships God.

With one exception, we see this same pattern of response in Mary's call from God. Mary first asks the "how" question. "How can this be since I am a virgin?" Whether the question is asked from anxiety, doubt, or curiosity, we cannot know. The angel's response is more measured to Mary than it had been to Zechariah. The angel characterized Zechariah's response as lacking in belief. The difference in response is suggestive that Mary's "How" question comes more out of anxiety rather than out doubt or lack of belief.

While Abram acts without hesitation upon the command of God, he and Sarah are not without some pause in this whole story either. When the three strangers come to affirm to Abraham, who is now ninety nine, that he will have a son, Sarah laughs and questions how she will bear a child in her old age (Genesis 18:13). The three strangers call Sarah and Abraham on the laughter as a lack of faith and then they reaffirm that surely it will come to pass in due season.

Gabriel answers Mary's "How" question quite directly. It will be through the action of the Holy Spirit. Then, Gabriel offers evidence through Elizabeth that with God all things are possible. In the case of Sarah, the mother is ninety years old. In the case of Mary, the mother is a virgin. In both cases, it is clearly evident that God is at work. Mary responds with, "Here am I, the servant of the Lord, let it be with me according to your word." There is no holding back now, but whole hearted commitment to the purposes of God.

Mary, who is now with child, goes to visit Elizabeth. Like Abram she has obeyed God. Upon Mary's greeting to Elizabeth, there is given to Mary a further confirmation of the promise; even as Abram received confirmation once he had arrived in the land. Elizabeth, through her own pregnancy, experiences confirmation of what is happening with Mary and responds with, "Blessed are you among women, and blessed is the fruit of your womb." Mary's response to this confirmation is to exercise her faith, like Abram's response, in the worship of God. Mary breaks out in song, "My soul magnifies the Lord" (Luke 1:46-55). At the end of Mary's song, she proclaims God's action through her is a fulfillment of God's promise made to Abraham. Matthew at the very start of his gospel records the beginning of the genealogy of Jesus with Abraham.

Finally, who is the child who is the focus of the promise? The child born to Abraham and Sarah is Isaac. Isaac is the beloved, only son of Abraham and Sarah born through the intervention of God. When this only son is twelve or thirteen, God will test Abraham and Isaac at Mt. Moriah (Genesis 22). When Mary's son, Jesus, is thirty three, he will be tested at Mt. Moriah as well.

Mary's child is the only Son of God, Jesus Christ. This parallel between Isaac and Jesus will be explored in the next chapter in detail. At this point let us simply note that Jesus is the fulfillment of the sacrifice that is prefigured in Isaac. Jesus, in fact, becomes the lamb that is offered by the God who provides a way of salvation for all who will believe. The promise of blessing to all the families of the earth made to Abram finds its fulfillment in Mary's son, Jesus! Isaac and Jesus are both children of promise. Both represent the promise of God is kept.

Lesson Plan for Study

Get acquainted - What was a big decision that changed your life?

I.   **The call of Abraham - Read – Genesis 12:1 – 9,**

     A. **What attracts your attention in the story?**

     B. **What do you want to know more about in the story?**

     C. **What is the promise in the story?**

     D. **Which promise appeals to you?**

     E. **What does God command?**

     F. **What must be left behind?**

     G. **Why Abraham?**

     H. **How does Abraham respond?**

     I. **What will God call you to do at 75 years of age?**

II.   **The call of Mary – Read – Luke 1:26 – 38, 55; Matthew 1:1**

     A. **What attracts your attention in the story?**

     B. **What do you want to know more about in the story?**

     C. **What is the fulfilment you see in the story?**

     D. **What is God's invitation?**

     E. **What is at risk?**

     F. **Why Mary?**

     G. **How does Mary respond?**

     H. **What is the promise of God to Mary?**

     I. **What does Mary need from the angel to help her in her faith journey?**

III. How do the calls of Abram and Mary interpret each other?

    A. What does the call of Abram say about the call of Mary?

    B. What does the call of Mary say about the call of Abram?

    C. What is the promise given to Abram that finds fulfilment in the call of Mary?

    D. What do these calls tell us about God's action in our lives?

    E. What do these calls tell us about people?

    F. How do Abraham and Mary see themselves?

    G. How does this challenge you to see yourself?

LESSON 5

The Sacrifice of Isaac and the Cross of Christ

Scripture

The Sacrifice of Isaac – Genesis 22:1 – 14

The Cross of Christ – Matthew 27:32-54; Mark 15:22 – 39;
Luke 23:33-47; John 19:17 - 30

Overview

Christians experience many challenges and difficulties in their lives. Certainly, one of those difficult challenges happens when Christians suffer pain and hurt in a broken world. We ask with complaint, "Why must good people suffer bad things?" The issue that is even more difficult to come to terms with is faced when Christians suffer pain and injustice precisely because they are Christians. The truth today is that around the world there are more martyrs for the Christian faith than during the first century of the church. We ask with complaint, "Why doesn't God protect those who love him from such injustices?" Such injustices, which seem to reflect a lack of protection, appear to be at odds with the very character of God.

What we miss in the midst of our feelings of injustice is that we live in the midst of a broken world. This world is not like the one which God created in the first place. Sin has broken this world, and it is out of sync with God. In a broken world, pain must be expected. The only way to right what is broken in the world will require confrontation and pain. That is a hard truth to face, but it is the reality of the faith.

Jesus gives expression to this truth in his Sermon on the Mount. In Matthew 5:10, Jesus says, "Blessed are those who are persecuted for righteousness' sake, for theirs is the kingdom of heaven." The scripture is clear. A Christian's faith will be tested. Such testing will not only be expected but will be a source of growth in a Christian's faith. Take a look at Romans 8:17-26, Philippians 3:10, Colossians 1:24, 2 Thessalonians 1:4-5. Peter also picks up the same theme that suffering ought to be an expectation and is a test of the believer's faith (I Peter 4:13; 5:10). Peter emphasizes that through suffering God's purposes will be realized in us.

This understanding of the role of suffering is the context for taking a look at two parallel passages of scripture. The first is the Old Testament story of the Sacrifice of Isaac. The story begs the question: what is going on here? What is God up to? How can Abraham possibly do what is asked of him? These questions cannot be fully answered apart from the New Testament story of the Cross of Christ.

There is an incredible depth of parallels between these two passages that underscore that God has a plan. God's vision is laid out in Genesis, and the fulfilment of that vision is seen in the Cross of Christ.

The first parallel relates to the place where both stories unfold. The land of Moriah, referred to in Genesis 22:2 as the site where Abraham was to take Isaac, is Jerusalem. Mt. Moriah will become the temple mount area where the temple will be built. On the northwest corner of the Herod period temple complex was the Antonia Fortress originally built to hold vestments used in temple worship. During the first century AD, the fortress was named after Mark Anthony and was used as the military command post by the governor when he was in Jerusalem.

So, when Jesus is brought before Pilate, it was at the Antonia Fortress next to the temple complex on Mt. Moriah. It was there that Pilate sentenced Jesus to the cross, and there he was beaten by the soldiers, and there the crown of thorns placed upon his head. The way of sorrows along which Jesus carried the cross led from the fortress and Mt. Moriah to Golgotha, the place of his crucifixion.

God is very specific in directing Abraham all the way from Beersheba, where he had pitched his tent in the south of Israel just north of the Negev desert, to Jerusalem in the mountains of Moriah. It will be a three day journey for Abraham to get from Beersheba to Mt. Moriah. There is something specific about this place that God wants to impress upon Abraham. The plan of redemption is already beginning to unfold.

To explore this plan as it unfolds in both the Old Testament and the New Testament, we will focus on the "who", the command, the response, the results, and the parallel symbols that we find in both texts. Finally, we will explore what both texts teach us about God.

First, let's take a look at the "who", the central characters in both texts. The son of the Genesis story is Isaac, the only son of Abraham and Sarah. Isaac is the son who has been the focus of the covenant between Abraham and God, and who represents the future of Abraham's descendants. Note the descriptive terms used in Genesis 22:2: "Take your son, your only son Isaac, whom you love."

The son in the New Testament story is also described in similar descriptive terms at the baptism of Jesus in Mark 1:11, "A voice came from heaven, 'You are my Son, the Beloved; with you I am well pleased.'" As Jesus explains in the upper room to the disciples, he is the focus of the new covenant that God is going to establish through the sacrifice of Jesus' blood upon the cross. At the cross, even a Roman centurion will acknowledge that this man was the Son of God.

The fathers in both texts include Abraham, the father of a multitude or many nations and Almighty God our heavenly Father. Father is the term Jesus most often uses in reference to God. Through the sacrifice of Jesus Christ, God will become the father of all who believe, and they will be called the children of God.

The command of God to Abraham was "take your only son, go to the land of Moriah (Jerusalem), and offer him there" (Genesis 22:2). At the transfiguration of Jesus, Elijah and Moses appeared and talked with Jesus about "his departure, which he was about to accomplish at Jerusalem" (Luke 9:31). In the garden of Gethsemane, we find Jesus praying three times that the cup of suffering and sacrifice would be removed from him. But at the end of each prayer is the statement of commitment, "not what I want, but what you want" (Mark 14:16). It is clear that Jesus is also under the direction and command of the Father. The place where he is to go for the sacrifice is also the land of Moriah, Jerusalem. The command requires sacrifice in both cases.

Why was a sacrifice commanded? Sacrifice in the case of Abraham affirmed a covenant between Abraham and God. Sacrifice was also a test of faith. Faith is tested to discover how reliable both parties to the covenant really are. Sacrifice was also made in order that sin could be forgiven. Sacrifice in these cases was to be done through the shedding of blood. Sacrifice is also implicit within the very nature of love. Expressions of love typically involve sacrifice of some kind as we are so vividly reminded in O. Henry's short story "The Gift of the Magi." In O. Henry's short story the husband sells his pocket watch to buy hair combs for his wife's hair, as she sells her hair to buy a chain for his pocket watch. Family is empowered by sacrifice as parents sacrifice for their children and for each other. Children will be called upon in later years to sacrifice on behalf of their older parents. This reminds us that the context of any discussion about sacrifice will, at its root, involve an expression of love. Certainly the love Abraham has for God and Isaac is seen here along with God's love for Abraham and Isaac along with Isaac's love for his father, Abraham, as well as his heavenly Father.

The sacrifice of Jesus upon the cross affirmed a new covenant between God and all who would believe in Jesus. The cross was clearly a test for Jesus. That is the message of the garden of Gethsemane. Jesus settled the issue in the garden where he sweats drops of blood before he faced the cross. The cross was endured and the blood of Jesus was shed for the forgiveness of sin. However, the cross is also an expression of love. In this case it carried an expression of the love of God for human kind.

Jesus makes it clear that he was a willing sacrifice. Jesus was not a victim of the Jewish or Roman authorities. He could have left Jerusalem at any point before the arrest. He clearly knew what was coming. On the way to the cross, Jesus could have called upon his power and glory and stopped the whole business right then and there. Within that same context, Isaac also appears to be a willing sacrifice or at least an accepting sacrifice. Remember, Abraham is one hundred and twelve, and Isaac is twelve. There is no way that Abraham is going to bind and offer Isaac as a sacrifice without at least the co-operation of Isaac.

When we consider the response of Abraham, we note that it was early in the morning when Abraham rose, saddled his donkey, and set out. It was a three day journey, but Abraham did not delay in starting out. To be sure, Isaac asks a question about where the lamb was, but as noted above, Isaac does not appear to resist his one hundred and twelve year old father. Isaac is obedient to his father and God.

Abraham trusts that God has a plan. He doesn't know what the plan is, but he trusts God, as indeed he had trusted God when he left Haran for the Promised Land thirty seven years earlier. Hebrews 11:17 – 19 suggests that Abraham's trust in God was such that he concluded that God was able to raise Isaac up, even from the dead. That of course was precisely the trust that Jesus had in the Father. The several times that Jesus predicted his coming death, he also predicted that on the third day God would raise him up. Even though Jesus makes that prediction three times before Holy Week, the disciples still did not see it coming. The resurrection caught them by surprise. Jesus believed in the resurrection going to the cross. He trusted the Father all the way.

The pictures that we have of Abraham and Jesus are the same picture of obedience. Jesus says, "Not what I want, but what you want." Abraham binds his son and places him upon the altar. As God witnesses the faithfulness of Abraham, he stops Abraham. As Abraham has told Isaac, God does indeed provide. A ram is suddenly seen caught in a thicket by its horns. The ram becomes the sacrifice, a substitute for Abraham's son. There are some similarities here between the ram and Jesus who is named at the beginning of his ministry by John the Baptist as the Lamb of God who takes away the sins of the world. Jesus has a crown of thorns placed on his head. The ram is caught in a thicket by his horns. A thicket conveys the image of tangled brush and thorns. Jesus becomes our substitute to save us from the penalty of sin.

The results of the test demonstrate that the covenant is reaffirmed. God affirms his blessing of Abraham. Abraham affirms his complete trust in God. Isaac experiences the covenant in a very personal way. Isaac discovers for himself again, in a very personal way, that God will provide.

Some of the other parallel symbols that we find include Isaac carrying the wood for the sacrifice, while Jesus carries the cross up to Golgotha. Isaac was bound by his father. Jesus was bound by the chief priest to be delivered to Pilate. The ram was pierced by a knife while Jesus was pierced with nails and a spear. God provided the ram, and God provides his Son in order to establish a new covenant. Abraham took two men with him on his journey to Mt. Moriah. They are left with the donkey as Abraham and Isaac go up the mountain. Jesus is taken to Golgotha with two other men who are also crucified.

Finally, both texts teach us that God will provide. Yes, we live in a scary world. There are difficult challenges that we will need to face, but God will provide. It will require faith, but the call is to trust in the Lord. It is the trust in the Lord promise that the prophet Jeremiah, in the face of exile, proclaims in Jeremiah 29:11-12. "For surely I know the plans I have for you, says the Lord, plans for your welfare and not for harm, to give you a future with hope. Then when you call upon me and come and pray to me, I will hear you."

Another major discovery within these stories that underscores the thought that God will provide is that God has a plan. Abraham and Isaac lived two thousand years before Jesus, yet we witness in the Abraham and Isaac story the plan for the redemption of human kind that will come to fruition in Jesus Christ upon the cross. God clearly has a plan that he is carrying out to redeem human kind. God is for us and desires the best for us.

Lesson Plan for Study

Get acquainted – What's difficult about the Christian faith for you?

I. **The Sacrifice of Isaac – Genesis 22: 1 – 14**

    A. What attracts your attention in the story?

    B. What bothers you most about this passage?

    C. Why was the sacrifice necessary?

    D. What is the point of testing?

    E. Who is Isaac? (Specific to what the scripture emphasizes)

    F. Who is being tested and why?

    G. What does God command?

    H. When and how does Abraham respond?

    I. What meaning do you see in the ram caught in the thicket?

    J. What is the primary message of the story?

II. **The Cross of Christ – Mark 15:22 – 39**

    A. What attracts your attention in the story?

    B. What bothers you most about this passage?

    C. Why was the sacrifice necessary?

    D. Who is Jesus? (Specific to what the scripture emphasizes)

    E. How does Jesus respond?

    F. Who is being tested and why?

    G. What correlations do you see between Jesus and the ram in Genesis?

III. **How do the sacrifice of Isaac and the cross of Christ interpret each other?**

    A. How do the sacrifice and the cross parallel each other?

    B. What is difficult in both stories?

    C. What is the central meaning of both stories?

    D. How does the setting bring the stories together?

    E. What do the stories tell us about the nature of God?

    F. Compare the responses of Isaac and Jesus. What ought to be the response of Christians today to the two stories?

    G. What perspective do these stories bring to the challenges of faith?

LESSON 6

THE GARDEN OF EDEN
AND THE GARDEN OF GETHSEMANE

Scripture

The Garden of Eden – Genesis 2:8-9; 15-17; 3:1-19
The Garden of Gethsemane – Luke 22:39 - 53

Overview

We live in a world with a vast variety of beauty all around us. Some of the most beautiful places my wife and I have enjoyed include: the Smokey Mountains of Tennessee, the road to Hana in Hawaii, the Sea of Galilee, mountain vistas from the village of Assisi in Italy, and the trees of Brown County, Indiana in the fall. Uppermost on my list are gardens with trees such as Cypress Garden in Florida.

Joyce Kilmer catches my feelings when he says, "Only God can make a tree," "A tree that looks at God all day, and lifts her leafy arms to pray."

I have found gardens to be quiet places that bring me closer to God and his creation. Gardens are places of growth and the marvel of God's gift of life in all of its infinite variety. In a garden, I find serenity and a wonder that also empowers my creativity.

Within the context of the variety of beautiful places that God has created upon the face of this world, we have a perspective from which to look at these two garden stories found in the Old and New Testaments.

The Lord God planted a garden in Eden and put the people he had created in the garden. Out of the ground grew every tree that was pleasant to the sight and good for food. It was vibrant with life. It was paradise. We learn that the man and the woman walked with God in the garden in the cool of the evening. It was a place of fellowship and communion with God. It was indeed paradise!

The man and the woman were to till the garden and keep it. The garden is not a maintenance-free place. The work of creation is an ongoing enterprise. The man and the woman are invited to participate with God in the wonder of his creation. At this point in the story there are no weeds and the ground is cooperative with Adam and Eve. All the productivity that was the possibility of creation was realized. That kind of work is a joy and rewarding. That kind of work suggests a cooperative relationship between the man and the woman and God and the garden in which they dwell. That kind of work should produce wonder at the scope of God's creation which they are invited to participate in and enjoy. The scene also suggests that God has given human kind a partnership relationship with Him in the care of this world He has created.

In the midst of this garden God planted the tree of life and the tree of the knowledge of good and evil. While the man and the woman could eat freely of all the other trees of the garden, there was one exception, the tree of the knowledge of good and evil. Thus temptation was also found to be in the garden.

"You shall not" seems to be a temptation that is hard for humans to resist. For human beings to have free will, they will of necessity always be plagued by temptations. Temptation is in the very nature of free will. You cannot have free will without having temptation to misuse that free will in relationship with others. Unique in creation, human beings were created with free will. To the man and the woman alone is given the command "You shall not." To these persons, created in the image of God, was given the limitation that true relationship always demands: you shall and shall not.

Also to be found in the garden is the betrayer, the tempter, the one who comes to lure the man and woman away from obedience to God. The tempter has his own agenda, and it is not God's agenda nor is it in the best interest of the man and the woman. The tempter's agenda is the same as he suggests to the woman a desire for power. So the snake says, "When you eat of it your eyes will be opened, and you will be like God." You will be in charge. Wherever there is temptation, there always seems to be a tempter, someone who would lure you away from what is best for you and betray you. Of course the temptation is never framed in that way. The temptation will always appear to benefit you at least in the short term. The tempter will most often appear to be a friend who is looking out for you and would not want you to miss out on this opportunity for power or enjoyment. But the tempter never has your best interest in mind, only his or her interest in mind.

One of the tools of the tempter is our dislike for limitations. Just tell a child no and watch the immediate reaction. Why can't I? Many times you will find a child testing the limits of what they can or cannot do. There seems always to be the desire to push the boundary just a little further. I'm not so sure that this behavior is limited to children. All you have to do is observe adults driving down an expressway with posted speed signs.

So the tempter asks, "Did God say, "You shall not eat the fruit of the trees in the garden?" The woman jumps to God's defense and says, "We may eat of the fruit of the trees of the garden, but you shall not eat the fruit of the tree in the middle of the garden, nor shall you touch it, or you shall die." While the woman defends God, she also makes the limitation more severe than it actually is. Nothing has been said about not touching the fruit. In our mind we often make limitations more onerous than they actually are. It is a reaction to our dislike of limitations in the first place.

Another tool of the tempter is doubt. The tempter's immediate response to Eve is to call God's word into doubt. The tempter says, "You will not die." In effect, he is calling God a liar. Then the tempter provides a reason for the lie and the seed of doubt. "God knows that when you eat of it your eyes will be opened and you will be like God, knowing good and evil." In one sense Adam and Eve already know good and evil. Good is following the command of God. Evil is disobedience of God's command. What has not happened is that Adam and Eve have not yet committed an evil act, and as result have not yet experienced evil the consequences of such action. Adam and Eve do not yet know quilt. Adam and Eve are innocent in their lack of knowledge about guilt and the devastation that guilt brings to a person's life.

When Adam and Eve do commit the evil act of disobeying a direct command of God, the first consequence they experienced is guilt and shame, and so they try to hide from God. Other consequences will follow, all of which reflect upon the broken relationships that are the result of sin. We see broken relationships between the man, the woman, and God: between the man and the woman, between the man and woman and creation itself. More broken relationships will appear as time goes on. When Adam and Eve know evil, they know brokenness, guilt and shame. In the knowledge of guilt, paradise is lost.

Can paradise be regained? What Adam and Eve fail to do in the garden, after their disobedience, is to admit their failure and ask for forgiveness. What would have happened in the garden in the cool of the evening, when God came to walk with them, if Adam and Eve had said, "God we ate of the fruit of the tree in the middle of the garden? We messed up big time and we are sorry, please forgive us." Could paradise have been regained through forgiveness? That question is not answered in the Garden of Eden. Because no one took any responsibility for their sin and each blamed each other, and the snake, and God himself for what happened, paradise was lost.

But we now come to another garden, the Garden of Gethsemane. It is a quiet place with olive trees and quiet nooks that invite rest, reflection, and prayer. Into this quiet garden at the foot of the Mount of Olives, Jesus came with eleven of his disciples. Jesus invites three of his disciples to come deeper into the garden (into the middle of the garden?) to pray with him. Into this garden the betrayer will come. Temptation is already there beneath the trees.

Jesus already feels the weight of temptation. The garden of Gethsemane is named for the olive press that is in the midst of the garden. An olive press is used to squeeze out the oil from olives that can be used for cooking, lighting the house, and to promote healing in wounds. A heavy stone weight is placed on the cracked olives and the oil is collected as it flows from the olives.

In the Garden of Gethsemane, Jesus knows what the command of the Father is. Jesus prays, "Father if you are willing remove this cup from me." Jesus knows what the cost of obedience is. The nature of temptation is that it is real and hard. This is not a walk in the park for Jesus. The scripture tells us that so heavy is the temptation that weighs down upon him that sweat became like great drops of blood being squeezed out from him. That description gives us a picture of the depth of the anguish Jesus was going through in the Garden as he wrestled with temptation. Jesus could have easily escaped the trial and the cross. After all, just beyond the Mount of Olives is the Wilderness of Judea. All Jesus had to do is simply walk away from Jerusalem and he would leave behind the cross with all its pain and humiliation.

Jesus adds to his pray each time he prays there in the garden, "Not my will but yours be done." Jesus accepts the limitation of his place. He is not the Father, but the obedient Son. Constantly throughout his ministry, Jesus is conscious of his filial responsibility to his father. Jesus always gave credit to the Father. Jesus continually directs worship to the Father. It is a limitation that Jesus does not appear to chafe under, but rather he rejoices in it. He is the Son not the Father, and he rejoices in their relationship. So Jesus prays, "Not my will but yours be done."

The Father responds to the declaration of dependence that Jesus makes, and an angel comes to strengthen Jesus there in the garden. Jesus does not go it alone. Throughout his ministry, Jesus has consistently gone to the Father for strength and direction. Jesus will not be left alone in the garden to struggle with temptation on his own when he declares his dependence upon the Father.

Now there are doubts to be sure. Three times he comes to the disciples, who are not praying but sleeping. Can these disciples really carry on the message? Will my sacrifice really accomplish the task? Can these weak, argumentative men really change? Yet, Jesus' response each time is to wake them up again and encourage them to pray.

Then the betrayer enters the garden. Why does Judas betray Jesus? We do not know. But if we were to ask Judas, he would likely have said this is for Jesus' own good. Jesus will thank me when it is all over and Jesus bursts forth with all the power of which he is capable and is crowned King of Israel and Rome is cast aside. Of course, there would be underlying currents of what was in it for Judas that would be defined in dimensions of power.

But Jesus takes the full measure of what is happening when he says, "Judas, is it with a kiss that you are betraying the Son of Man?" Judas, are you trying to say you love me, that you are my friend, and yet you betray me? Jesus recognizes the betrayal for what it is, even if Judas cannot. At the same time, Jesus affirms his limitation, his place, as the Son of Man. Jesus says no to the temptation to reject the cup of suffering and will drink it to the dregs.

In the garden the faithful Son will be obedient to the command of the Father, even to death upon the cross where his blood will flow out. In this garden can paradise be regained? The hint of the answer is seen in the backdrop as a sword is drawn and an ear is cut off and the consequences of sin continue to spin out of control. It is at that point Jesus yells, "No more of this!" The cycle of evil does not need to continue. The cycle of evil and its consequences can be stopped and healed.

Then Jesus touches the servant of the high priest's ear and heals it. In the garden forgiveness is offered. Is that a foretaste of the healing to come as Jesus sheds his blood upon the cross? Is not paradise regained when we look upon the cross and confess our sin and ask for forgiveness? The battle with temptation is won in the garden. Jesus, the faithful Son, will lay down his life so that the brokenness of sin may be healed in our body and soul.

In saying "no" to temptation, and "yes" to the Father's command, Jesus is correcting the failure in the Garden of Eden. When Jesus calls from the cross upon the Father to forgive them, he means we human beings created in the image of God. In those actions of obedience and requesting forgiveness for us, Jesus is carrying out what was promised in the Garden of Eden. The head of the serpent was struck as Jesus rejects the serpent's way of betrayal of the Father. Sin and disobedience don't have to be the way of man. The Son of man has been obedient even unto death. Indeed in that death, full of pain and suffering, the serpent bruises his heel, but on the third day Jesus will rise from the dead and open the gates of paradise to all who will believe. Death, the penalty of sin, cannot keep him who has not sinned for he has been obedient to the Father all the way. His death and shed blood then become the sacrifice that breaks the power of sin and the deceit of the betrayer for all those created in the image of God as they look upon the cross with faith. The image of God in which human beings were created is revealed in all its purity and power. We can respond to the love of God in love and faithfulness.

What do these passages of scripture say to our own struggles with temptation? In the face of temptation, Eve listens only to the serpent. She does not appear even to talk to Adam about it until the fruit is already picked. Jesus, in the face of temptation, goes to the Father in prayer. Jesus brings friends along, even though they fail him when it matters. The Father sends an angel to give Jesus strength. It matters to whom we turn when we are facing temptation. In the wilderness Jesus turns to the Word of God. Here in the garden he prays to the Father and it makes all the difference in the outcome.

In the face of temptation, Eve distorts the command of Father. Jesus, In the face of temptation, wants to be clear about what the command of the Father is. Adam and Eve are seduced by the vision of power to be like God. They become confused about who they are. Jesus is clear about who the Father is and who the Son is. The vision of Jesus is to do the will of the Father. Eve mistakes the serpent for a friend who is looking out for her, instead of seeing him as the betrayer that he is. Jesus is clear about who is the betrayer, and is not confused by the friend who offers a kiss. When we are not clear about who we are, it is easy to get confused about who our friends are.

Let's be clear, temptation is not sin. Jesus was tempted, but did not sin. To keep from falling into sin, it is important to know what to do in the face of temptation. This dialogue between the choices of Adam and Eve and the choices that Jesus made, gives us clear directions of what we should we do in the face of temptation. In the face of temptation: be clear about the commands of God, don't be seduced by visions of power, remember who you are, and know who your friends are. The way to be clear about who we are, is to talk it over with our creator. Talking it over with the creator also addresses the other three directions that we learn from Jesus. This suggests that the fifth direction of Jesus is the one he epitomizes in the Garden of Gethsemane. In the face of temptation, go to the Father in prayer. Jesus was so intense in his praying that his sweat was like drops of blood.

Let's take this discovery one step further. Temptation is not sin. Sin is giving in to temptation. We have all done that, even as did Adam and Eve did. What then? What should we do in the face of sin? Three things suggest themselves out of the failure of Adam and Eve and the positive example of Jesus. First, take responsibility. Adam and Eve turned to the blame game instead of acknowledging their sin. You cannot deal with sin if you refuse to accept responsibility for what you have done. Second, ask for forgiveness. Asking for forgiveness, acknowledges both that we have done wrong and expresses sorrow, repentance, for the wrong we have done. Third, seek fellowship with God. God came down to the garden in the cool of the evening fully aware of what Adam and Eve had done. God was offering fellowship and reconciliation, but Adam and Eve hid, as if it were possible to hide from God. Hiding from God is in reality is hiding from ourselves the truth of what we have done. Seeking out God, to confess our sin, does not surprise Him about our sin, but it does reveal the sorrow of our hearts that we have sinned and disappointed both Him and ourselves. Jesus entered the Garden of Gethsemane, instead of climbing the Mount of Olives and escaping the cross, was for the expressed purpose to make it possible for people created in the image of God to be reconciled to God so that we might regain paradise. These three actions in the face of sin hold the key to our regaining paradise.

Lesson Plan for Study

Get acquainted – What is one of the most beautiful places you have been?

I.   **The Garden of Eden – Genesis 2:8-9,15, 3:1-9**

    A.   What attracts your attention in the story?

    B.   What bothers you about this passage?

    C.   Why a garden?

    D.   Why are Adam and Eve placed in the garden?

    E.   Why is the tree of the knowledge of good and evil in the garden?

    F.   What is the temptation?

    G.   What are the reactions of Adam and Eve?

    H.   How does God handle the disobedience?

II. **The Garden of Gethsemane – Luke 22: 39-44**

    A.   What attracts your attention in the story?

    B.   What bothers you about the story?

    C.   Why a garden?

    D.   What was temptation like for Jesus?

    E.   What doubts might Jesus have had?

    F.   What is the critical moment in the garden for Jesus?

    G.   What do you think was going on for the Father as Jesus is praying?

    H.   How do you account for the behavior of Judas?

III. How do the Garden of Eden and the Garden of Gethsemane interpret each other?

  A. What do the two stories tell you about the nature of temptation?

  B. Where does temptation come from?

  C. What do you learn from the two stories on how to handle temptation? How to handle sin?

  D. What does the Garden of Eden say to the Garden of Gethsemane?

  E. What does the Garden of Gethsemane say to the Garden of Eden?

  F. Can Paradise be regained? How? Why?

LESSON 7

THE BURNING BUSH
AND THE ROAD TO DAMASCUS

Scripture

The Burning Bush – Exodus 3:1-5, 11-14, 4:1, 10, 13
The Road to Damascus – Acts 9:1-5, 10-6

Overview

I was standing in line at a church potluck dinner, and I was just making small talk with another member of the church who owned a small business in town. I had heard that Randy was planning on building a new facility and relocating his business to a more visible location in town. My question was simple enough. "Randy what are you going to do with your old building?" Randy's answer came as shot out of the blue that stunned me. "Why that's going to be the location of the new United Methodist Hispanic Church in town." Randy's words shocked him as much as they had shocked me. The thought of his old building being used as a church building had not struck him until he uttered those words. I had been working with the United Methodist Hispanic Church in town for a couple of years and they were badly in need of a new location. Several efforts had been explored earlier that had not worked out. I had become a bit frustrated whether anything could really be done for this small neighboring congregation. My response to Randy was, "We need to talk."

What happened over the next 9 months was nothing short of amazing. I had never seen Randy's old facility before our conversation. But the next day as I toured the facility with Randy, a vision for the church began to take shape before my eyes complete with worship space, kitchen, and Sunday school space. I sketched out the vision and then met with the pastor of the Hispanic church. There was a whirlwind of committee meetings, prayer meetings, and drawing up plans, getting various approvals, securing funds, buying building materials, and pulling together work teams. Nine months later that conversation at a church dinner had become a reality as the El Mesias United Methodist Church dedicated its new facility to the praise of God. They celebrated with a worship service and a church carry-in dinner for themselves and all their friends who had helped make this moment a reality. It was the first facility they had owned themselves. They had worked alongside Anglos to turn an old business building into a church.

It was an amazing time when everyone involved in the project saw God bringing everything together to accomplish his purpose. I was astonished at how several different factors that had begun earlier suddenly all came together at the same time to remind us that God was in charge.

God's call is like that. What appears to be impossible or beyond our doing can be accomplished if that is the purpose and desire of God. It is the kind of thing that takes your breath away when you view it over the vantage point of time.

That is a perspective I would like us to keep in mind as we take a look at these two passages of scripture in this chapter. Both scriptures come seemingly as a shot out of the blue, completely unexpected. Both scriptures are a call from God that will have a life changing impact not only upon the person called but upon the people to whom the messenger will be sent. The people to whom the messenger is sent understand themselves as people who are hopelessly ensnared and lost; people whom God has forgotten, or so it seems.

Both of these passages of scripture are very rich with meaning in their own right, but when placed together, I believe they speak to us even more about the nature and purpose of God who is persistent and purposeful. There are several parallels in the structure of these passages that call for our attention. How does God get the attention of his messenger? How is God identified? Who is the messenger? What reassurance does God give the messenger? Who is the helper that facilitates the calling? What are the results of the encounter?

How does God get the attention of his messenger? Moses is leading the sheep of his father-in-law beyond the wilderness when a flame of fire appears out of a bush. The bush is blazing but not consumed. When Moses turns aside to take a closer look at the bush, he hears a voice calling, "Moses, Moses." God has Moses' attention. Saul is riding his horse to Damascus leading a group of men who were on their way to the city to arrest Christians. A light from heaven flashed around Saul and knocked him off his horse. Saul hears a voice calling, "Saul, Saul, why do you persecute me?"

In both cases each messenger is completely unaware that God is trying to get their attention. These callings do not come at the end of a vigil or a session of prayer, but literally it comes out of the blue while Moses and Saul are busy about other things. In both cases there is flash of light or a fire that suddenly gets their attention. It stops Moses in his tracks and knocks Saul off his horse. Both also hear their name called twice. They are known; even though they have no idea who it is that is talking to them. While both callings seem to come out of the blue, the reality is that there is a backdrop behind the call of both men. The backdrop behind both callings is the result of long planning at least by God.

As Moses responds with "Here I am," God identifies himself to Moses as the God of Abraham, Isaac, and Jacob. Moses hides his face afraid to look at God. Later, Moses will ask more specifically, "What is your name?" God answers Moses saying, "I AM WHO I AM." On the other hand, Saul upon hearing his name being spoken and the charge that is laid against him, also asks, "Who are you, Lord?" Jesus identifies himself with the "I AM" of God saying, "I am Jesus, whom you are persecuting." The men who are with Saul see no one and Saul is blind even though his eyes are open.

God identifies himself first in both cases in terms that the messenger can understand. For Moses it is in terms of the God of his ancestors. In Saul's case it is Jesus the one Saul is persecuting. Both respond with hiding their face or going blind in the face of God. Both immediately know the truth of who is speaking to them. Both are given commands by God about what they are to do. In both cases the plans that are given are drawn out further as a dialogue goes on between God and the messenger.

The encounter with God happens a bit different in these two cases, but the effect is the same.

Moses is immediately told what he is to do and why God is concerned that this action needs to be taken. Moses has a number of objections which we will look at later, but the dialogue that takes place between Moses and God over the mission begins to spin out in a way that Moses can understand better. As the message develops, Moses comes to a clearer sense of who he is and who God is!

Saul, on the other hand, is only told what his next step is. "Get up and enter the city and wait for further instructions." Saul will wait three days, but those three days are spent in darkness without eating or drinking. Those three days for Saul are a time of reflection and waiting upon the Lord in prayer. The specific instructions for Saul's mission will be given to another to relay to Saul and then it will be confirmed by the Lord directly to Saul.

The missions that both Moses and Saul are given also directly relate to the identity of who God is as well. Moses is to go to Pharaoh with the message from God, "Let my people go!" Moses is to name the name of the Lord before Pharaoh. In this message of "Let my people go," God is reminding Egypt of their broken covenant with Joseph and God. God is on the side of the oppressed. God will not forget the covenant he made with Abraham and with Joseph. God has seen the misery of his people. He has come to act; to deliver them from oppression and bring them to a land flowing with milk and honey. God intervenes in human history. He comes to right wrongs. While God is sending Moses to declare to Pharaoh the message, "Let my people go!", God is clear, He will go with Moses.

Saul's mission is to bring the name of the Lord before Gentiles and kings and before the people of Israel. The mission will be difficult. Saul will suffer a lot in accomplishing the mission. His life, like the life of Moses, will be threatened on many occasions. Ananias confirms to Saul that it was the Lord Jesus Christ appeared on Saul to the road. It is the same Lord Jesus Christ who has sent Ananias to restore the sight of Saul and to facilitate Saul's receiving the Holy Spirit. Saul is being sent, but he will not be going alone, God in the person of the Holy Spirit will be going with him.

God is Lord not only of Israel but also of the Gentiles. Kings are also answerable to God. Confronting kings with the name of the Lord is a dangerous work as Moses discovered before Pharaoh. Saul will discover the same danger before Governor Felix, King Agrippa, and later Emperor Nero. God is a realist in telling Saul that this mission will cost Saul. Through Saul, God is going to intervene in a powerful way throughout the known world. The message of the good news of Jesus Christ is for all the earth.

Who is the messenger that God has called? Moses is the messenger from God to Egypt who will facilitate Israel's escape from slavery. Moses is the name given to the three month baby by an Egyptian Princess, the daughter of the Pharaoh, meaning, "I drew him out of the water." We never learn Moses' Hebrew name, which we presume he was given at birth. Moses new name will relate him to the Egyptians to whom he will later challenge on behalf of God. Moses will lead Israel through the wilderness for 40 years to the Promised Land. Moses became uniquely prepared for his calling long before the burning bush experience. Moses was a Hebrew child, but was raised in the palace and was taught the ins and outs of palace protocol. The preparation shifts to a new venue when Moses goes out among the Hebrew and sees one being missed treated. Moses murders the Egypt overseer and then must flees Egypt. Moses' new venue will be in the wilderness of Midian as a shepherd where he learns the skills of leading and traveling in the wilderness. This is precisely the skill set that Moses will need as the messenger of God.

Saul is called to be the messenger of God to the Gentiles, kings, and Israel. The encounter with Jesus on the road to Damascus changes Saul's name to Paul. Paul will facilitate the establishment of churches from Antioch to Rome with his longest times spent at Ephesus and Corinth. Paul will stand before Felix, Festus, and Agrippa in Caesarea. After Paul appeals to the emperor, he will finally go before Nero in Rome in the center of the empire. Saul/ Paul is also uniquely prepared for his role in his assigned mission by God long before he takes the road to Damascus. Saul is born a Roman citizen at Tarsus. Saul reads and writes both in the Greek language and in Hebrew language. Saul is his Hebrew name. Paul is his Greek name. Saul is also a Jew who has been educated in the Jewish law by the famous teacher Gamaliel. Saul also has a trade of tent making. Saul arrived in Jerusalem after the resurrection of Jesus. Upon his arrival in Jerusalem, Saul will be present when Stephen presents his witness to the Lordship of Jesus Christ. Saul held the coats of those who threw the rocks at Stephen even as this first martyr cried out for the forgiveness of those who persecuted him. Stephen's last sermon before the rocks flew included an extended recitation upon the call of Moses and the rebelliousness of Israel to the word of God delivered by Moses in the wilderness. In Stephen's message, the rebelliousness of Israel before Moses is clearly being compared to the rebelliousness of Israel to the word of God delivered by Jesus. All of that was heard and seen by Saul before he headed to Damascus to carry out the persecution of other followers of Jesus. After the death of Stephen, Saul launches a campaign of persecution against the church and is on his way to Damascus in pursuit of that purpose when the light from heaven knocks him off his horse. As a zealous trained Jew who is also a Roman citizen and a tent maker, Saul is uniquely positioned both in the Jewish world and the Gentile world.

In both of these men, we see God at work in their lives long before they are called to their particular missions preparing them in unique ways to be his instrument to accomplish their mission. John Wesley would call this "Prevenient Grace." "Prevenient Grace" is the grace of God that comes before we are even aware of God's action in our lives. John's perspective paints a picture of God who not only intervenes in human history, but who does so with a plan and purpose.

When Moses hears the mission that God has for him, his response is to say, "Who am I that I should go to Pharaoh? God's answer to Moses is "I will be with you." In other words, it is not who you are Moses, but who I AM. Moses then wants to know God's name and is given the name I AM WHO I AM. Then Moses is reminded that I AM has been the God of Abraham, The God of Isaac, and the God of Jacob. God had changed the name of Jacob to Israel. Now Moses is to call together Israel the nation, the descendants of Jacob (Israel), and tell them that God has seen their misery and he will deliver them from slavery and bring them to the land flowing with milk and honey, the Promised Land. Moses comes up with several other objections which God answers until finally Moses says, I have no eloquence. God who gave speech says again, I will be with you and with your speech. Then God sends Aaron to be Moses' helper. God has already sent Aaron out to meet Moses. Aaron is to be told what to say by Moses and Aaron will then be Moses' spokesman.

Ananias is the helper that God sends to Saul. Ananias has been told by God what it is that Saul's mission is and what Saul needs. It is Ananias who baptizes Saul. Upon his baptism Saul is filled with the Holy Spirit. After baptism, Saul's name is changed to Paul. God will now be with Paul as he declares the name of God before Gentiles and the house of Israel. It is through the direction of Jesus Christ and the power of the Holy Spirit that Paul is sent out to turn the world to God and set people everywhere free from sin to live in relationship with the Father and come at last to the Promised Land.

Aaron will be Moses' helper throughout Moses' mission to lead Israel out of captivity and into the Promised Land. After the initial stage of leading Israel out of captivity, there are many other helpers who God brings to Moses particularly after the advice of Moses' father-in-law, Jethro. Most notable among those were Joshua, Caleb, and Hur. In the case of Saul, Ananias is the early helper who helps transition Saul into the faith and guides Saul's early preaching efforts in Damascus. After that, we hear no more about Ananias, but there is a succession of helpers or fellow workers in carrying out Paul's mission. Most notable among these are Barnabas, Silas, Luke, Timothy, and Titus. These are just a few mentioned, but there appears to be a whole team of persons who gather around Paul. They travel with Paul for a time and then are sent off on a mission that supports the work that they are all doing together. It illustrates another pattern of what God typically does in our lives. His mission for us is seldom a lone wolf project, but he will call helpers around us to aid in the accomplishment of the task set before us. Succession is important to God as well. Joshua will be the successor of Moses. Timothy, Titus, and many others are the successors to the work and mission of Paul.

Another element that is a part of both of these stories of Moses and Saul is the emotional response of both Moses and Saul to their encounter with God. Moses is intrigued by the burning bush and moves closer and finds himself on holy ground. Holy ground is any ground where we encounter God. Upon hearing the mission Moses can identify with the need, but at heart it also triggers his fear. Moses is a wanted man in Egypt as guilty of murder. That is why he left Egypt in the first place. When Moses considers going back to Egypt, he is filled with anguish and resistance, which takes some time for God to overcome. Saul is knocked off his horse by a blinding light from heaven and is faced with the question of "Why are you persecuting me?" Saul would have had an immediate fear reaction to this question. He is currently on a mission to arrest Christians, but even more bothersome for Saul is the witness of Stephen as Stephen was stoned to death while Saul held the cloaks of those throwing the rocks. The next three days of blindness and fasting will be a soul searching encounter with God for Saul. Attached to the experience of both Moses and Saul in their encounters with God is a deep sense of unworthiness. Moses question of God is "who am I that I should go to Pharaoh?" Saul sees himself as the least of the Apostles. That sense of unworthiness will play out by giving all the credit of what is accomplished through them to God. The person who responds to God with "I knew you would need me, O Lord" is probably unsuited for a mission in which the Lord is the one in charge.

What are the results of the encounters that Moses and Saul have with God? Moses leads Israel out of captivity and to the Promised Land fulfilling a part of the promise of God to Abraham. God had promised to make of the descendants of Abraham a great nation and give to them the land which he had promised. Indeed Israel is now a numerous people who have been freed from slavery and are a nation whose God is the Lord and who live according to the laws of God. The struggle as Israel moves to become a nation will be defined in their faithfulness or lack of faithfulness to God. Another part of the promise of God to Abraham was that he and his descendants would be a light to the nations. The mission of Saul, who becomes Paul, is directed precisely at this fulfillment. Paul brings the light of Christ to the Gentile world into the very heart of the empire. Like Moses, Paul will lift up the name of the Lord before everyone he encounters, despite threats upon his life and all the suffering he must go through. The name of the Lord will be proclaimed, and it will mean life to all who receive it. Whereas Moses establishes the nation of Israel to bear the name of God, Paul will help establish the church as a witness to the gentile world that will name the name of Jesus as a witness to God's love for all who have been created in his image. In both Moses and Saul, God is fulfilling his covenant with Abraham.

As we look at the road to Damascus through the lens of the burning bush there are truths that we learn about God. God has a deep passion that all the peoples of the earth know him and his love for them. God desires that all the earth to know and honor his name. God hears our cries and sees our misery when we live apart from him. God acts through people to make a difference in our lives, free us from slavery to sin, and give us eternal life with him. When God acts through people, he prepares them uniquely for the mission that he has in mind before they are even aware of what God is about. When they finally become aware of God and of God's passions and desires, they hear God's call upon their lives. As they respond to God's call upon their life, God acts again to empower them through the Holy Spirit and brings additional people around them to share in the work that is be done. God is always about community. Relationships matter to God.

We also learn something about the people that God calls in these stories as well. Both Moses and Saul had been involved in murders. Both were hard driving persons who before their calls took matters into their own hands and went off in the wrong direction. Both needed to have their enthusiasm yoked to the guidance of God. No one is beyond God's redemption and renewal.

God uses the simplest things to get our attention: a bush that is suddenly aflame, a light flashing down on the road we are traveling, a line waiting to get to the table at a carry in, or your own simple moment when you hear your name spoken by God. It is God calling you by name to uphold his name in a lost and confused world full of slavery and addictions that destroy life. There are excuses aplenty that we could offer, but God's presence is sufficient. We then can stand with Paul before King Agrippa and declare that we have not been disobedient to the heavenly vision, and we have declared the name of the Lord who is a light to Israel and the Gentiles.

Robert Browning wrote, "Earth's crammed with heaven, and every bush aflame with God. But only those who see take off their shoes. The rest sit round and puck blackberries."

Lesson Plan for Study

Get acquainted – Describe a time when you felt God calling you to do something specific?

I. **The Burning Bush – Exodus 3:1-5, 11-14, 4:1, 10, 13**

    A. What attracts your attention in the story?

    B. How does God get Moses' attention?

    C. What do you learn about Moses in the story?

    D. What do you learn about God in this story?

    E. What makes ground holy?

    F. What is God's purpose or mission? Why?

    G. What is Aaron's role in the story?

II. **The Road to Damascus – Acts 9:1-5, 10-16**

    A. What attracts your attention in the story?

    B. How does God get Saul's attention?

    C. What do you learn about Saul in the story?

    D. What do you learn about God in this story?

    E. What is God's purpose or mission? Why?

    F. What is Ananias's role in the story?

III. **How do the Road to Damascus and the Burning Bush interpret each other?**

    A. How do these two stories parallel each other?

    B. What is the central meaning of both stories?

    C. What do you learn about God's calling of people?

    D. How does the story of the burning bush clarify Saul's mission?

E. How does the road to Damascus clarify the mission of Moses?

F. What do you learn about the passion of God in these stories?

G. How does the road to Damascus fulfill the mission of Moses as it is echoed through the promise to Abraham?

H. How are you called to lift the name of the Lord before people?

I. How does the Lord get your attention?

LESSON 8

THE TEN COMMANDMENTS AND THE BEATITUDES

Scripture

The Ten Commandments – Exodus 20: 1 - 21
The Beatitudes – Matthews 5: 1 - 12

Overview

In the family in which I grew up, there were very definite rules of the family that my sister and I were expected to follow. Failure to follow the rules of the family would be met with significant consequences. Failure to follow the rules even more would raise the question about whether you were acting as a part of the family. Failure to follow the rules wasn't just disobedience, but it was a betrayal of whom you were, a Wortinger.

Five of those rules come immediately to mind. First, we would be going to church every Sunday for both worship and Sunday school. We will not squirm, and we will pay attention and be involved. We typically also went to a mid-week service. The worship of God and the fellowship of the church were important to my parents. Both of my parents became Christians when they were in their twenties. They taught their children that the church and faith in Christ meant life to them. The second rule was to respect your parents. My parents modeled that behavior in the way they respected and honored their own parents. It went without saying that respecting your parents included obedience. The third rule was to tell the truth. If you lied about something when questioned, the consequences for lying would be worse than what was being asked about in the first place. In short, you were expected to own up to any failure and not deny responsibility or blame the behavior on someone else. The fourth rule was to clean your plate. Food was not to be wasted. Your mother went to a lot of work to prepare the food for you. Your father worked hard to make the money to purchase the food for your meal. As a result of all this effort, your responsibility was to clean your plate. The fifth rule was that there would be chores. We were a family and everyone was expected to do their part, not only in keeping your own room clean and tidy, but chores that would benefit the whole family such as drying the dishes, carrying out the garbage, and in winter carrying out the ashes from the furnace. An element of chores that went much further than just doing the chores was that you were always expected to give your best effort. Goofing off or doing a shoddy piece of work was not acting like a Wortinger.

Now, every family has rules that define them as a family, not necessarily these five that characterized my family. Some families will have more and some will have fewer rules. However, typically, the clearer a family is defined, the more the rules will be aimed at shaping the family and providing the family with a definitive identity. To have no rules for the family is to have no identity or family as a consequence. To have no identity as a family is to invite dire consequences for the various members of the family.

That is the context for taking a look at these two scriptures. Exodus 20: 1 -21 gives us the rules for the family that was Israel who had just received their freedom from slavery in Egypt and who were on their way to the Promised Land where they intended to become a nation. They would become a nation with a particular identity. Three thousand years later, the Jews people still are a people with an identity.

A case in point illustrates the issue. The ten northern tribes of Israel went into captivity having lost touch with their identity as outlined in the Ten Commandments. They are the lost tribes of Israel. They became lost to history. The two southern tribes also go into captivity at a later time. The southern tribes, however, double down on their identity rooted in the Ten Commandments. They confessed that their state of captivity was caused by their failure to be obedient to the law. As a result, in captivity, Israel recommitted itself to the law and developed the synagogue system for the learning and studying of the law, the rules of their relationship to God.

Matthew 5: 1 -12 gives us the rules, the expected behaviors, of those who would be followers of Jesus and become members of the Kingdom of God. In both cases, the identity of both of these groups is defined in family terms. In both groups, God is seen as their heavenly Father and the head of the family. In both groups the purpose of the rules is to guide the appropriate behavior in relationships within the group. Both sets of rules spell out the relationship one is to have with God and with others. One of the major differences in these two sets of rules is that one states these relationships negatively, that is what you shall not do if you are a member of the family is defined. The other set of rules is stated positively in terms of what it means to be a part of the family, which is to be blessed.

Both sets of rules are spoken upon a mountain: Mount Sinai in the case of the Ten Commandments. In the case of the Beatitudes it is a mountain by the Sea of Galilee. Both sets of rules are proclaimed by God.

It is the Father who speaks the rules to Israel as they gather at Sinai and then writes them by his finger on a tablet of stones at Mount Sinai. The Father delivers these rules on tablets of stone just after Israel has been freed from slavery. Israel is on the way to the Promised Land. As the Father proclaims these rules, Israel is formed into a nation with an identity. As they are faithful to their identity by obeying the rules, they will find success as a nation and as a family. A failure to maintain their identity will result in their failure as a nation.

It is the Son who speaks the rules to the disciples and the multitude who have gathered at the mountain by the Sea of Galilee early in his ministry, just after the calling of the disciples, according to Matthew. To be faithful to these rules, to these traits of the Kingdom of God, is to be blessed. To be faithful to these rules is to be salt and light which is the theme of Matthew 5: 13-14. As Jesus talks about salt and light he is talking about identity. There is no mistaking salt and light. If salt has lost its taste, it is no longer salt. If light doesn't shine, it isn't light. The message of the Beatitudes given on the Mountain is that these positive traits give identity to the members of the kingdom of heaven.

In the early medieval period a very common depiction of Jesus showed Him holding a book with writing in a similar pose that is often associated with Moses coming down from Mount Sinai with tablets of stone which have the finger writing of God upon them. Jesus in that time period was portrayed as a second Moses, a second law giver.

In comparing the Ten Commandments to the Beatitudes, their similarities are found in two groupings about relationships. One grouping is about our relationship to God, and the other grouping is about our relationship to others.

In the Ten Commandments, the first four commandments reference our relationship to God. You shall have no other gods before me. You shall not make for yourself an idol. You shall not misuse the name of God. Remember the Sabbath day, and keep it holy. The implications of these four commandments are that God is to be number one in our lives. He is our primary relationship. There is to be no substitute for God. God is holy and his name is to be treated with respect. There is to be a regular pattern to life where we regularly turn to the Holy God in worship.

The foundation for the new nation of Israel is to be God. The nation does not and cannot exist apart from him. Israel's very life flows from the one who created human kind and who called Abraham and who delivered Israel from slavery.

In the Beatitudes, the first, the fourth, and the sixth seem to reflect on our relationship to God. The first is "Blessed are the poor in spirit, for theirs is the kingdom of heaven." The phrase the "poor in spirit" refers to humility. Our relationship to God requires coming into his presence with humility, not with a sense of demand or pride. Pride and the whole "I" center is what are at the heart of sin and the kind of behavior that will always disconnect us from God. Humility is approaching God as the creator. He is Lord. This Beatitude reflects the first two commandments that want us to be conscious of the dynamics of our relationship with God. The first Beatitude and the first two commandments point to the position that God is to have in our lives. We do not come before him as equals. He is Lord. The first Beatitude also points us to the promise that is ours when we recognize that God is creator and that we are the created by stating... "For theirs is the kingdom of heaven." This is the entrance into the community of God's people, his kingdom.

The fourth and sixth Beatitudes are concerned with the genuineness and depth of our relationship with God himself. "Blessed are those who hunger and thirst for righteousness" is a plea for a passion about the things of God. Righteousness is God's great desire. Those who want righteousness so intensely that they hunger and thirst for it have identified with the purposes of God. Hunger and thirsting for righteousness are at the heart of worship. Worship cannot be genuine without it. Worship is not about a form, but it is about substance. We really want God and his righteousness not just <u>in</u> our lives, but <u>in control</u> of our lives as hunger and thirst can control us. His name is that sacred to us.

"Blessed are the pure in heart" speaks to single mindedness and lack of duplicity in our worship of God. It suggests that we are whole heartedly focused on God, and there are no disguised motives. We come with thanksgiving that he is our God, and our love for him is genuine gratitude for his creative and redeeming love that has been at work in our lives. Worship and making the day holy are about being a living sanctuary for the presence of God not only in our lives but also in our world. The concern for purity is reflective of God who is pure and holy. His name will be kept pure and holy by us. That same concern for genuineness and depth of relationship is reflected in the third commandment about misuse of the name of God and the fourth commandment about Sabbath worship. Both commandments are about worship and the sacredness of God's name.

Note as well that the two promises connected with the fourth and sixth Beatitudes also add depth to the third and fourth commandments. The promise of the fourth beatitude is "for they will be filled." Our passionate desire for God is answered by his passionate desire for us. When we gather for worship and when we honor the Sabbath day, we are met by the presence of God who fills us with his Spirit and his love. The promise of the sixth beatitude is "for they will see God," which is the desired outcome of worship. Again the promise is that we will be met by God himself. It is God's desire that we see him. He desires to reveal himself to those who will be genuine in their relationship with him, who will seek him out in worship, and honor his name.

The blending of the first four commandments and the first, fourth, and sixth Beatitudes give a more complete picture of what God desires in our relationship with him, and the promise that such a relationship holds out for us as citizens of the kingdom of heaven.

The last six commandments deal with our relationship with others. The fifth commandment has a tighter focus upon the family and the relationship between children and parents. This commandment is also stated more positively and with a promise that is more reflective of the style of the Beatitudes. The last five commandments have a broader application to our relationship with others. These commandments are in the form of you shall not. You shall not murder. You shall not commit adultery. You shall not steal. You shall not bear false witness. (lie) You shall not covet. Any breach of these five commandments would also break down the community and nation. If people are going to live together in harmony as a single nation, these commandments must be kept. The foundation of the nation of Israel is at stake. The Founding Fathers of America were absolutely insistent upon this. The only hope for a democratic nation to survive was if it was a moral nation, reflecting upon the Ten Commandments as the foundation of that morality.

The second Beatitude is a kind of bridge beatitude in that I can see it applying both to our relationship with God and others. Particularly in its promise it is suggestive of our relationship with God. "Blessed are those who mourn, for they will be comforted." In our relationship with God, it is suggestive of our mourning for our sins in repentance. It is the prayer of the penitent heart. The promise that is paired with this Beatitude is "for they will be comforted." The promise for the penitent sinner is that he will be met by the forgiveness of God. The second Beatitude deals with the reality that human beings are sinners. We have in fact already broken the commandments. How can our relationship with God be restored? In the Old Testament the issue of forgiveness is addressed immediately after the proclamation of the Ten Commandments with the making of an altar for sacrifice. The point of the altar of sacrifice was showing repentance.

The second beatitude as it relates to our relationship with others connects at the point of defining mourning as empathy. When we mourn with others, it connects us to others and to God who also mourns with us and meets us in our pain and loss.

The word "comfort" implies presence with another. Mourning with others is an indication of true community where people are united with each other and with God. Community is what it means to be a part of the kingdom of heaven.

The second beatitude clearly has a vertical relationship to God and a horizontal relationship to others. The cross is also an example of the vertical and horizontal with the vertical taking precedent.

The third, fifth, seventh, and eighth Beatitudes also deal with our relationships with others and the principles that undergird the kingdom of heaven. Blessed are the meek. Blessed are the merciful. Blessed are the peacemakers. Blessed are those who are persecuted for righteousness's sake. It is hard to imagine any of these behaviors being compatible with murder, adultery, stealing, lying, or coveting. In fact these behaviors express themselves in ways that shape a person into a citizen of the kingdom of heaven who would not break the last five commandments. The meek will deal with others gently and be conscious of the needs of others. The merciful are those who are willing to extend God's mercy to others giving expression to the key ingredients of community: love and forgiveness. The peacemakers carry out the task of reconciliation. Peacemaking is a further extension of mercy and becomes an active force in the community to foster peace and reconciliation. It is the behavior that we see in Jesus as he reconciles us to the Father through the cross. The cost of peacemaking is illustrated in the eighth beatitude and by the cross. It is the very work of God himself. Those who are going to persist in righteousness despite persecution illustrate the endurance that is required of citizens of the kingdom of heaven who are still living in the midst of an imperfect world where God's reign is not yet complete. While the commandments tell us what will break community apart, the beatitudes tell us what will build community. Both perspectives help us to better understand the behaviors needed in a community of God's people who live in a world that is often in rebellion against God's rule.

The four promises associated with these four beatitudes also add to our understanding of the community whose identity is rooted in God. "For they shall inherit the earth" has an interesting correlation. To inherit the earth is suggestive of the promise of the Ten Commandments that Israel would dwell in the Promised Land. The Promised Land that the citizens of the kingdom of heaven look forward to is that place where the Father is its light and center.

"For they will receive mercy" and "for they will be called children of God" and "for theirs is the Kingdom of God" all underscore the interaction of the citizens of the kingdom of God with God himself. Our interaction with others, particularly as we give expression to the character of God, also brings us into relationship with God. The whole point of the Ten Commandments was to create a community of people who not only live in relationship with God but do so in a way that God will be seen by the world through them. That is also clearly the vision that Jesus is casting in the Beatitudes as well.

In summary, the Beatitudes add an important positive perspective to the Ten Commandments that takes us further into what builds a community of God's people. The Beatitudes also give us a fuller vision of the promises that God fulfills for the citizens of the kingdom of heaven. On the other hand, the Ten Commandments are a necessary negative warning about what breaks community. The Ten Commandments are very concrete in helping us understand that what is at risk is our relationship with God. The Ten Commandments also defines our very identity. There are both negative and positive rules for the family of God which can guide us into the Promised Land where we can live forever in his light.

Lesson Plan for Study

Get acquainted – What were the family rules you were taught as a child?

I.   **The Ten Commandments – Exodus 20: 1-17; 18-21**

   A.   What attracts your attention in the story?
   B.   What does it mean that God is jealous?
   C.   What is the point of the Ten Commandments as a whole?
   D.   Which commandment is easiest to keep? Hardest?
   E.   What is the point of the first four commandments?
   F.   What is the point of the last five commandments?
   G.   In verses 18-21, what do you learn about the people?
   H.   What do verses 18-21 suggest is the need of the people?

II. **The Beatitudes – Matthew 5: 1-10; 11-12**

   A.   What attracts your attention in the story?
   B.   What is the point of the Beatitudes as a whole?
   C.   How is the blessed approach different than the "thou shalt not" approach?
   D.   Which Beatitude is the easiest to live out? Hardest?
   E.   What word strikes you in the Beatitudes? What does it mean?
   F.   How do the beatitudes portray our relationship to God?
   G.   How do the beatitudes portray our relationship to others?
   H.   What perspective do verses 11-12 add to the Beatitudes?

III. How do the Ten Commandments and the Beatitudes interpret each other?

    A. How do the Commandments give definition to the Beatitudes?

    B. How do the Beatitudes fulfill the Ten Commandments?

    C. What do the Ten Commandments and the Beatitudes teach about God? About people? About relationships?

    D. What is righteousness?

    E. What is the Kingdom of Heaven?

    F. Where do you feel challenged by the rules of the family of God?

LESSON 9

THE CALL OF ISAIAH
AND THE CALL OF THE DISCIPLES

Scripture

The Call of Isaiah – Isaiah 6:1 - 9
The Call of the disciples – Luke 5: 1 - 11

Overview

Where do you experience the presence of God in your life? For me that question has an assortment of answers. I experience the presence of God most regularly in worship, particularly in the service of Holy Communion. In those times I find my attention is focused toward God. In that attentiveness, I find that God is indeed there ready to engage me. The same thing is true when I am intentionally attentive to God when I read scripture or pray. However there are also times when I am surprised by the presence of God when I come across a particularly beautiful scene while traveling or while walking along a beach and watching the waves rolling in against the backdrop of a setting sun. Then too, there are times when my mouth hangs open in awe at the miracle of a birth or the realization that God has been at work in some area of my life of which I was totally unaware except in later reflection on how a blessing came to pass.

All of that is suggestive that there are a number of ways in which we can become aware of the presence of God in our lives, but certainly one way which we might cultivate our awareness of God's presence is intentionally paying attention. My experience and my faith tell me that God is present continually in our world and is at work to accomplish his purposes. God is at work in the majestic and the mundane. But God doesn't autograph his masterpieces in the way that an artist might. The work of God is seen through eyes that have become attuned to him. Being attentive to the presence of God is the disciplined act of a believer. The failure to believe robs us of the eyes to see what is right before us. In my experience some of those who claim to be agnostic do so because they had a vested interest in believing there is no evidence of God. If they were to believe in the reality of God, then they would have to change their behavior.

The lack of attentiveness also robs us of the sensitivity that believing eyes require. One of the problems of our busy and noisy lifestyle in modern society is that we can walk around almost oblivious to what is happening around us because we are so focused on ourselves and the mundane in our lives. The disciplines of worship, participating in the sacraments, reading scripture, and prayer can be ways in which we can practice attentiveness that can reward us richly in the life of the spirit. These are ways of stopping and breaking through all the confusing noise around us and listen for the one voice that knows our need and can give direction for our lives.

But God is not left with just waiting for us to begin to pay attention. God can and does shout at us at times to gain our attention. Sometimes those shouts just take our breath away, and we behold the grace and love of God that is directed at us. We find ourselves wondering how this is possible. At other times the shout of God presses down on us as we struggle with the demands and tragedies of life that are too much for us when we insist upon going our own way in the world. In both cases God is shouting, waving his arms, trying to capture our attention. Yet some will still turn a deaf ear and a blind eye and persist in their own direction through life focused only upon self.

God attempts to gain our attention, first, because of his love for us. We have been created in his image. He wants to live in relationship with us, and He has indeed planned an eternity for us to share. However, beyond God's love for us, or perhaps because of God's love for us, God attempts to attract our attention in order to invite us to join him in his purposes in the world. God's invitation is to work with him, to be his partner in something that needs to be done in the world - something that has eternal significance. The full scope of what God has in mind is seldom seen by us in the beginning or at all. But the implications of even the simplest of acts when seen against the backdrop of eternity can be staggering.

So the question, "Where do you experience the presence of God in your life?" is an invitation to be reflective. It is an opportunity to stop and think about when God's attention has been directed toward you. It is an overwhelmingly audacious thought that begs the question, "Who am I that God should turn his attention toward me?" Yet it also begs the question, "Who is this God who wants to engage me in relationship?" These questions are the blessing of becoming aware of the presence of God in one's life. That awareness gives answers to both questions that will of necessity change one's life.

It is against this backdrop that we will be looking at two persons who encounter God within the scriptures. One is the prophet Isaiah who is one of the gigantic pillars of faith in the Old Testament. The other is the disciple Peter, who is a gigantic pillar of growing faith in the New Testament. There are actually four disciples in this passage of scripture from the New Testament, but Peter is the lead spokesman and so our focus will be upon him. Their stories in Isaiah 6: 1-9 and Luke 5:1 – 11 are remarkably similar in some ways, and the differences between their stories serve to underline themes that are suggestive of the ways in which God seeks to encounter and interact with humans today.

In Isaiah 6:1, Isaiah says, "I saw the Lord!" It is clear that this encounter that Isaiah has with God is the turning point of his life. As Isaiah tells us "I saw the Lord," he also gives us the context of when and where this encounter took place. The when and where of their encounters with God has a bearing on both the stories of Isaiah and Peter.

For Isaiah, the "when" is in the year that King Uzziah died. The year was 742 BC, but more to the point, the year that King Uzziah died was a year of turmoil for both the nation of Judah and for Isaiah personally. The reign of Uzziah had been the most prosperous for Judah since the reign of King Solomon. In the later years of his life, Uzziah became a prideful man. Uzziah went to the temple to offer sacrifice unto the Lord himself, instead of allowing the priest to offer the sacrifice as required by the law of God. Uzziah was struck in judgment by the disease of leprosy. Uzziah will die as a leper, and his son comes to the throne when his father contracts leprosy. Judah is headed for trouble and everyone knows it. Isaiah resides in Jerusalem and is a member of the court. The whole tragedy around the end of Uzziah's reign troubles Isaiah. It is in the midst of this trouble, when the future looks bleak for Judah, that Isaiah saw the Lord.

The "when" for Peter is not quite as dramatic, but it is in the midst of frustration. Peter and Andrew along with James and John were washing their nets after a very disappointing night of fishing. They had thrown out their nets and gathered them in repeatedly throughout the night, but they had caught nothing. Professional fishermen like these four seldom came home completely empty handed. Now, they were engaged in the task of washing their nets, cleaning them from the bits of seaweed ensnarled in the nets from their fruitless night of net casting. They knew full well, it was going to be another long night on the sea tonight if they were going to feed their families. Here are four tired, frustrated fishermen trying to get things ready for the night when a teacher commandeers Peter's boat to speak to the crowd. After he is done speaking, the teacher suggests they move out into deeper water to catch fish. Here is a teacher. Peter has to wonder, what business does a teacher have telling me, a professional fisherman, how to fish. Fishing was done at night or late evening and early morning and not in the middle of the day! Yes, Peter was frustrated, tired, and more than a little irritated.

It seems that when we are in turmoil, frustrated and perhaps at the end of ourselves, that God can get our attention. Certainly it appears that it is easier to get our attention then when life is going well and we are full of ourselves. That at least seems to be a commonality for Isaiah and Peter.

The "where" of these encounters however is quite different. Isaiah has gone to the temple. The temple is certainly a place where one might expect to encounter God. Yet, those who go to the temple or church for reasons other than worshipping the Lord of all creation may very well miss him even in that place. It is so easy to get preoccupied with other things that it is easy to miss why this building was built in the first place. Isaiah had seen that recently as he witnessed King Uzziah come to the temple so wrapped up in his own pride and self-importance that the king was oblivious to God's presence until he was struck with leprosy.

The "where" for Peter is on the Sea of Galilee far from the temple. The Sea of Galilee was the site of Peter's daily work where the odor of fish was heavy in the air. Washing nets was a dirty smelly job. A working fishing boat is really not the kind of place where you would expect God to show up. However, the Sea of Galilee was where people had gathered to hear good news, and good news was proclaimed that day. Would we expect God to show up at our work place? Would we be embarrassed if he did?

However, the biblical record is that God encounters people in all kinds of settings. Moses was caring for sheep in the wilderness. Jeremiah had gone down to a potter's house. Ezekiel was in exile. Jonah was in the belly of a whale. Saul was riding a horse to Damascus. Matthew was at his tax collection booth and Zacchaeus was up a tree. There is no one particular place of encountering God. Yes, there is Samuel and Isaiah in the temple and Daniel and Nathaniel at prayer, but far more encounter God as they are going about their daily lives.

Before we leave the where question, there is one additional point to which we need to pay attention. There is a sense of volition on the part of both Isaiah and Peter. Isaiah goes to the temple in the midst of his need. Was he seeking God's presence? What expectations did Isaiah have that day as he went to the temple? Peter moves out into the deeper water at the urging of Jesus. Clearly, Peter is not excited about going out into deep water. Yet, he does move the boat into deep water and casts his net from the boat. Peter does what Isaiah had done. He put himself in a place where he might encounter God. What was it that Jesus had said to the crowd that made Peter willing to follow the directions of Jesus? What did Peter expect as he went out into deep water?

My own experience is that my own expectation helps prepare the way for God's action. At the very least it increases my awareness and my attentiveness to what is happening in me as well as around me.

The other question that we can ask both Isaiah and Peter is "How do they encounter God? Isaiah says he saw the Lord high and lifted up sitting on a throne. Isaiah goes on to describe the majesty of God. There is a sense of awe and power that sweeps over Isaiah. In my mind's eye I see Isaiah on his knees as the majestic display of the glory of God unfolds around him. Peter realizes that he is in the presence of God when he sees the incredible impossibility of nets bulging to the breaking point with fish and both boats so loaded down with fish that they were beginning to ship water. It is at that moment that Peter realizes that this is no ordinary teacher seated in his boat. This man Jesus was none less than God himself. Peter can do nothing else but fall to his knees as he too is swept away with the awe and power of the presence of God.

When they encounter God, there are two things that immediately crash in upon Isaiah and Peter. First, God is holy and his glory fills the whole earth. There is power here that is beyond comprehension. God is Lord! The second thing that grabs both Isaiah and Peter is their utter unworthiness. They both are very conscious that they are sinful men standing in the presence of a holy God! Isaiah says, "Woe is me! I am lost, for I am a man of unclean lips." Peter says as he sinks to his knees, "Depart from me, Lord, for I am a sinful man." Both men are overcome with the fear that sin brings when it is exposed to the light.

However, the key to both of these stories occurs at precisely this point as both men are on their knees conscious of their separation and sin before God. In the next few verses in both passages, we see a change that takes place in both men that takes them out of their fear and sets them on their feet with a mission of purpose that will change the rest of their lives. Take a close look at what happens in each case.

In the case of Isaiah, upon his confession of unclean lips, God acts. An angel takes a coal from the altar with a pair of tongs and touches the lips of Isaiah. A pronouncement is made, "Your guilt has departed and your sin is blotted out." Isaiah experienced forgiveness in an intimate and personal way. Isaiah knows God has acted to forgive him and now Isaiah stands in the assembly as God discusses the need for a messenger. The man who moments before is sinking to his knees in fear, conscious that he is lost, is now holding up his hand to get noticed by God volunteering to be

God's partner in the work that God is about. That is an incredible turnaround that is initiated by God's action. That action of God finds a response coming from Isaiah, and Isaiah becomes a new man.

The same kind of change takes place in Peter. As soon as Peter falls to his knees begging Jesus to depart from him, Jesus acts. Peter has confessed his sin and now Jesus tells Peter, "Do not be afraid, from now on you will be catching people." In other words, Peter you do not need to fear God, you are forgiven. In fact Peter, I have a job for you. It is then that we see Peter and the others leaving their nets behind to follow Jesus. The focus of Peter is changed by his encounter with Jesus. His world is no longer about fish. He leaves the greatest catch of fish he has ever captured in his nets behind to follow Jesus.

The flow of action in both stories is the same. There is a confession of sin which is followed by God's action of forgiveness and invitation. The invitation of God is to a relationship. One aspect of that relationship is an invitation to be God's partner in his mission in the world. The pattern is the same in both the Old Testament and the New Testament. In the New Testament, we see God's action to forgive upon the cross. But we see God's action toward forgiveness in the Old Testament as well. Isaiah experienced it in the form of a coal from the altar in the temple. But the whole function of the temple in the Old Testament was to facilitate the meeting of God and the people. The Lord created a place where the people would acknowledge their sin and he would forgive.

Certainly this is the pattern preached by John Wesley. God preveniently makes his presence know which initiates an awareness of sin and need. That confession of sin is met by the action of God in forgiveness and justification. The forgiven person is invited into relationship where he might become not only a disciple but a friend and a partner. The pattern of God's action in the life of Isaiah and Peter can be the action of God in our lives today.

The movement of God in our lives is always toward relationship. God's movement in our lives is invitational, to become involved in what he is doing in the world. Inherent in this flow of God's work in our lives is insight into the very nature of God. God is actively at work in the world constantly. He is actively engaged and interested in his creation for which he has a purpose and a plan. God is always looking for partners in his work. He has a passion for sharing what he is about. He also has a passion for reconnecting with the people he created in his own image. He desires relationship with us and is willing to forgive upon a person's recognition and confession of their sin and their separation from him that sin causes.

Let me make one further comment on the relationship of God's invitation to get involved in his mission. To Isaiah, who had been a member of the court of the king of Judah, comes an invitation to represent the king of all the earth as the king's spokesman. It is the kind of task that Isaiah was familiar with. It fit Isaiah. Isaiah is personally known by God and the strengths of Isaiah will be used. On the other hand Peter is a fisherman. Peter's invitation to get involved in the ministry of Jesus is an invitation to fish for people. Peter knows fishing but the object of

Lesson Plan for Study

Get acquainted – Recall a time when you experienced the presence of God?

I.   **The Call of Isaiah – Isaiah 6:1 – 9**

    A.   What attracts your attention in the story?

    B.   When does Isaiah experience the presence of God?

    C.   Where does Isaiah experience the presence of God?

    D.   How does Isaiah experience God?

    E.   What is Isaiah's response to his experience?

    F.   What accounts for the change in Isaiah's response from verse 5 to 8?

    G.   What does Isaiah learn about the nature of God?

    H.   What does Isaiah learn about himself in this encounter with God?

II.   **The Call of the disciples – Luke 5:1 - 11**

    A.   What attracts your attention in the story?

    B.   When does Peter experience the presence of God?

    C.   Where does Peter experience the presence of God?

    D.   How does Peter experience the presence of God?

    E.   What is Peter's response to his experience?

    F.   What accounts for the change of Peter's response from verse 8 to 11?

    G.   What does Peter learn about the nature of God?

    H.   What does Peter learn about himself in this encounter with God?

III. How do the calls of Isaiah and the disciples interpret each other?

    A. How does the call of Isaiah interpret the call of the disciples?

    B. How does the call of the disciples add to the call of Isaiah?

    C. What do you learn about the nature of God from these two calls?

    D. What do we learn about the when and where of our own potential experience of the presence of God from these two calls?

    E. What do these calls help us understand about God's expectation of us in our interaction with him?

    F. What might we learn about ourselves in an encounter with God?

LESSON 10

THE SACRILEGE OF NADAB AND ABIHU AND THE CLEANSING OF THE TEMPLE.

Scripture

The Sacrilege of Nadab and Abihu – Leviticus 10: 1-11
The Cleansing of the Temple – Matthew 21:12-16

Context

One of the arguments, that is given many times, suggesting that the Old Testament and the New Testament do not belong together is that the character of God in the Old Testament is one of a harsh judgmental God, while Jesus is loving and forgiving. The problem with the argument is that the characterization made of both Jesus in the New Testament and the God of the Old Testament is exaggerated in both.

Yes, the God we see portrayed in the Old Testament has expectations and is judgmental. Sin by its very nature is destructive. God does not want human kind ruled by sin. However, the Old Testament also portrays God as loving and reaching out to human kind in forgiveness and desiring reconciliation. While Adam and Eve are ushered out of the Garden of Eden, God does make for them clothes as they are sent out. Repeatedly in the Old Testament, God is pictured as forgiving and providing a place and a method to find forgiveness, when a person was repentant. In fact, it can be argued that the judgment of God is designed to move people to repentance so that God might forgive and restore them in relationship to Him. The action is more of a loving father, than a wrathful God eager to zap the sinner.

Likewise the picture of Jesus in the New Testament is exaggerated in the argument. Yes, Jesus is loving and forgiving. However, Jesus also has a judgmental and harder side. Jesus speaks against the Scribes and Pharisees (Matthew 23). In several of Jesus' parables there is a judgmental element which says a line has been crossed. I find the comment at the end of the story of the ten bridesmaids, "And the door was shut," to be positively chilling (Matthew 22:1-14; Matthew 25, Luke 16:19-31). The central event which draws this contrasting picture of Jesus is his cleansing of the temple (Matthew 21:12-16). The account is given in all four gospels. In Matthew and Luke, the timing is the same day as the triumphal entry into Jerusalem. In Mark's gospel, the cleansing is the next day after the triumphal entry. John places the timing for the cleansing of the temple at the very beginning of Jesus' public ministry.

There is a clear parallel between Jesus cleansing the temple and the Old Testament story of Nadab and Abihu that is referred to at least seven times in the Old Testament. Both stories revolve around the issue of worship before God and the need for a holy, pure place of worship. This parallel can help us understand that the character of God is the same whether we see him portrayed in the Old Testament or portrayed in Jesus in the New Testament. Jesus is clear on this point as he responds to Philip in the Upper Room. "Have I been with you all this time, Philip, and you still do not know me? Whoever has seen me has seen the Father" (John

14:9). The insistence of Jesus is that the Father we glimpse in the Old Testament is the same Father Jesus has come to make known.

Overview

What makes you angry? That list may be long, but typically there is something that leads the list - something that gets under your skin every time that will always upset us. Lying is one of those things for me. Lying frustrates me and makes me angry. I have experienced persons who have lied to my face as well as those who have lied about me behind my back. Those are painful situations that are hurtful on a personal level. I find myself always in a situation of making decisions related to my family, decisions about the church for which I had responsibility, decisions in regard to the community and the nation in which I live. When someone lies to me or distorts the truth, they make it harder for me to make a responsible decision. One of the frustrations that I find in our world today is the extent of distortion, if not out-right lies, that we find everywhere, about almost everything. Ascertaining truth these days is a difficult, but necessary quest. I value those persons who are truthful and distance myself from those who are not.

I raise this question as context for asking the question of what angers God. There is most certainly more than one answer to that question. Yet, the two passages of scripture that appear as parallels here are both related to one issue that makes God angry and which calls forth his judgment. These two passages are both in the context of worship. You will also remember that the first four of the Ten Commandments relate to worship of God. Both passages help us to understand what is involved in worship and what is at stake in worship.

Both the Leviticus story and the Matthew story are very brief glimpses that leave us wanting more information. Yet both stories are referred to numerous times in the rest of scripture. The Leviticus story is referenced three times in Exodus, two times in Numbers and twice in I Chronicles. That number of references suggests a very important issue. The Matthew story is also found in all three of the other gospels, again suggestive of an important issue.

The timing of both stories is interesting and connected. In Leviticus, the tragedy of Nadab and Abihu occurs immediately after the inauguration of the priesthood in Leviticus. The worship of God by the nation of Israel had just begun. The Ten Commandments had been given, and the rules for worship and sacrifice had just been established. At that point something went wrong. Nadab and Abihu were killed as a result. It is clear in the conversation that Moses has with Aaron that this not just an accident. It is clear that the two sons of Aaron have intentionally done something wrong in their worship before God.

In Matthew and Luke Jesus cleanses the temple immediately after his triumphal entry into the city with the shouts of "Hosanna, blessed is the one who comes in the name of the Lord!" still ringing in the streets of Jerusalem. Matthew brings those hosannas into the very courts of the temple. Jesus comes to the temple with the eyes of the crowd upon him. In Mark the cleansing is the next day. John picks up the same theme of preparation of the temple for the coming of the King but places the cleansing at the beginning of Jesus ministry.

The central point that both passages address is worship including the importance of worship to God and the necessity of worship for human beings. Worship gets at the very heart of God's desire to be in relationship with those he created in his own image. That relationship in worship must be clear about who the created are and who the creator is. That relationship gets confused at times and the created take on a greater role than is appropriate for them.

The story of Nadab and Abihu is short on details, but a few things are clear. Nadab and Abihu had just been ordained along with Aaron and their younger brother as priests who were to serve before God offering sacrifices on behalf of the people and for themselves. They were ordained for servanthood. The flow of the story seems to suggest that servanthood did not set well for them. They had just witnessed their father Aaron lift his hands in blessing upon the people and the fire of the Lord had consumed the burnt offering as the people all fell upon their faces in worship and adoration of God, almighty.

It is at this point that we see Nadab and Abihu each taking up their own censers. They put fire and incense in their censers to show themselves also offering fire before the Lord. Was this an attempt to focus the attention of the people upon themselves? Were they trying to put themselves on an equal footing with Aaron and Moses? We do not know what their motives were. All the text tells us for sure is that this was an unholy fire that was being offered and that this offering had not been commanded by

God. In other words they were acting on their own out of their motives.

The scene is reminiscent of the offerings made by Cain and Abel. Abel's sacrifice was accepted and Cain's sacrifice was not. The passage doesn't tell us clearly what the difference between the sacrifices really was, but the implication is that it had to do with their motives in making the sacrifice. Sacrifice was not an act contained within itself, but sacrifice was a way of expressing commitment and devotion to God. To offer a sacrifice to God with impure motives is a sacrilege. Such sacrilege offends the righteousness of God. Psalm 24:3-4 tells how we should come before the Lord in worship. "Who shall ascend the hill of the Lord? And who shall stand in this holy place? The answer rings out from the Psalm: "Those who have clean hands and pure hearts, who do not lift up their souls to what is false, and do not swear deceitfully."

It is clear that Nadab and Abihu do not have pure hearts in their worship. Moses reminds Aaron of the words of the Lord. "Through those who are near me I will show myself holy, and before all the people I will be glorified" (Leviticus 10:3). God expects His priests to be Holy. God will not accept challenges to his authority. He is Lord. He is holy. To worship the Holy One, purity and singleness of mind are required. Clearly Nadab and Abihu appear to have mixed motives in coming before the Lord. Worship is a sacred act that is not to be played with or to be made common or unclean.

Psalm 50:23 tells us how to come before God in worship. "Those who bring thanksgiving as their sacrifice honor me; to those who go the right way I will show the salvation of God." To bring thanksgiving is to come before God with gratitude. Nadab and Abihu do not appear to come before God with gratitude for their roles as servants before God. They are not content to fade into the background, but they seek out the limelight.

The result is that fire from the Lord consumed them and they died. To come before God in worship is a serious business that demands a pure heart. The restriction that Moses communicates to Aaron about mourning gives us a hint at the extent of God's anger with these two priests. The number of times that these two are spoken about in later scriptures as examples of what not to do also speaks to God's seriousness about worship.

Keep in mind that a regular worship pattern was just being established for the new nation. For worship to be corrupted right from the beginning was sure to lead the new nation down the wrong path. In fact, failures in worship would plague Israel until they are taken into captivity again. The writer of Chronicles clearly understands the Babylon captivity as God's judgment upon Israel's failure of real worship. The prophets Amos and Isaiah are also clear that worship is more than going through the motions, but it is a matter of the heart. They proclaim the coming judgment caused by a failure of worship of the heart.

God's judgment comes across loud and clear. There is that which is wrong and will bring judgment.

Jesus enters the temple in Jerusalem proclaiming the judgment of God. He announces the wrong. The temple was to be a house of prayer, a place where people could encounter a holy God. Jesus is quoting the prophet Isaiah. The full quote from

Isaiah 56:7 says, "For my house shall be called a house of prayer for all peoples." Jesus' specific concern is for Gentiles - for those who do not yet know God.

Note as well that Jesus views prayer as a central aspect of worship. Prayer is communication with God. Prayer allows us to hear the voice of God as well as make our needs and concerns known. In Leviticus, prayer glorifies God. He is Lord. In Psalm 50, worship is gathering in God's presence to offer thanksgiving. Prayer is heart to heart and goes beyond the formalities of ritual and sacrifice.

The Court of the Gentiles was the outer court of four courts which lead successively into the interior of the temple. It was the only area of the temple in which a Gentile could enter. But in this outer courtyard is where the tables for the money changers and the dove salesmen were setup. The money changers were there because Gentile coins needed to be changed for temple coins for offerings inside. Gentile coins typically had the graven image of an emperor or ruler upon them and thus they were inappropriate for temple worship. People coming to the temple to sacrifice did not always bring their sacrifice with them on a long journey and waited till they got to the temple to buy a dove or a lamb. The result of all this for the courtyard would be considerable racket and confusion with all the haggling and animal noises that would be going on. This would be the impression of what worship was all about for the Gentile who could go no further into the temple.

The implication of Jesus is that the transactions that took place in this outer courtyard were stacked against the visitor. Not only is Jesus saying this courtyard too noisy for prayer to

Almighty God, He accuses the priests of making the court into a den of robbers. The accusation challenges the holiness of the temple. The Messiah has entered the Holy City to bring salvation, but the very temple of God has been corrupted. Again, timing is key aspect of this parallel.

Jesus responds by overturning the tables and the seats of those who are selling. John says Jesus made a cord of whips to drive both the salesmen and the sheep and cattle from the temple. El Greco painted a rather dramatic depiction of this scene with Jesus lying on the whip to the offending persons. Certainly the whole scene communicates a sense of anger and judgment from Jesus about the failure of worship in the temple.

Jesus is immediately confronted by the chief priests and scribes who are angry at both what Jesus has done and what the crowd is saying about Jesus. Jesus responds to them quoting scripture that reflects God's desire for worship. The conflict between Jesus and the chief priests will lead to the cross within the week.

Matthew sees, in this conflict between Jesus and the priests, the coming judgment that Israel is calling down upon itself. In these verses Jesus curses a fig tree that is all leaves and no fruit. The fig tree was often used as symbolic of the people of Israel. The judgment upon the tree is that it withers at once because of its failure to provide fruit even though it looked good with lots of leaves. Mark also links these two passages of scripture together. Luke links the fig tree story two chapters later along with Jesus prediction about the destruction of the temple.

Clearly Jesus is acting out judgment and declares that a more encompassing judgment is coming because of the failure of genuine worship at the temple. You cannot read any of the gospels around the cleansing of the temple and conclude everything is alright with God. There is wrong that brings out judgment upon the people created in the image of God. The failure of worship is the failure of reconciliation - the failure to enter into a meaningful relationship with one's Creator. The failure of worship is a warning that needs to be taken seriously today as well. Worship is so important because it defines the relationship between God and his people. Because people are created in his image, the people who try to live without God are most certainly headed for disaster. If worship is missing in our life, judgment is inevitable because we are neglecting what is central to our make-up.

In the story from Leviticus and the story of Jesus cleansing the temple there is consistency regarding the emphasizing of the place and importance of worship in our relationship with God. Both stories point to the place of worship that God has commanded and prepared for the worshipper to come for prayer, praise, and to find forgiveness. In Leviticus, the setting is the Tabernacle. In Matthew, the setting is the Temple that Herod had built. Both stories are clear that the failure of genuine, pure hearted worship brings the judgment of God upon the people. Both scriptures also give us some clues about what worship should involve. The picture that both scriptures give us of God the Father who we meet in the Old Testament and the picture of God the Son that we glimpse in Jesus are consistent with each other.

Lesson Plan for Study

Get acquainted – What makes you angry?

I. **The Sacrilege of Nadab and Abihu – Leviticus 10: 1-11;**

    A. What attracts your attention in the story?

    B. What bothers you in this story?

    C. What more would you like to know about this story?

    D. What do you learn about the worship of God in this story?

    E. What does it mean to treat God as holy?

    F. What did Nadab and Abihu do wrong?

    G. How do you distinguish between the holy and the common?

    H. How does the timing of this story effect its meaning?

    I. How are we to come before God in worship?

II. **The Cleansing of the temple – Matthew 21:12-16**

    A. What attracts your attention in the story?

    B. What bothers you in this story?

    C. What more would you like to know about this story?

    D. What do you learn about the worship of God in this story?

    E. What does it mean to treat God as holy?

    F. What did the money changers and dove salesmen do wrong?

    G. What does this story tell you about what God wants?

    H. How does the timing of this story effect its meaning?

    I. What is the role of prayer in your private and public worship?

III. How do the sacrilege at the tabernacle and the sacrilege at the temple interpret each other?

    A. How does the tabernacle sacrilege interpret the actions of Jesus?

    B. How does Jesus at the temple interpret what happened at the tabernacle?

    C. What do you learn about God from these two stories?

    D. What do these stories tell you about the nature of worship?

    E. How important is worship?

LESSON 11

THE LORD IS MY SHEPHERD AND I AM THE GOOD SHEPHERD.

Scripture

The Lord is my Shepherd – Psalm 23
I Am the Good Shepherd – John 10: 11 – 18

Context

The context for chapters eleven and twelve are the "I Am" statements of Jesus as recorded in the Gospel of John. The "I Am" statements also relate to the holy name of God as it was given to Moses at the burning bush: "I Am who I Am." Moses was to tell the Israelites, "I Am has sent me to you" (Exodus 3:14). John, as he records the seven "I Am" statements in his gospel, does so with the clear purpose of illustrating "that Jesus is the Messiah, the Son of God, and through believing you may have life in his name." (John 20:31) Each of the "I Am" statements builds off of images of God that were well established in the Old Testament.

The seven "I Am" statements in John are: "I Am the bread of life." (John 6:48) "I Am the light of the world." (John 8:12) "I Am the door." (John 10:9) "I Am the good shepherd." (John 10:11) "I Am the resurrection and the life." (John 11:25) "I Am the way, the truth, and the life." (John 14:6) and "I Am the true vine." (John 15:1) John adds an eighth "I Am" in the book of Revelation: "I

Am the Alpha and the Omega," says the Lord God, who is and who was and who is to come, the Almighty." (Revelation 1:8)

The "I Am" statements are invitational in nature, inviting the believer into a relationship with Jesus. The "I Am" statements also point to the Father's relationship with Israel as illustrated throughout the Old Testament. Chapter eleven will illustrate that parallel between the Old Testament image and "I Am the good shepherd." Chapter twelve will develop the parallel between the Old Testament image and "I Am the bread of life."

Overview

My wife and I have two orange tabby cats, Sunny and Sparky. They are very responsive to my wife's voice. If she calls, they will come running. If she is dishing up some food for them, they are right there rubbing up against her, each other, and the furniture. When we leave the house, they will generally escort us to the door. When we return home, they will have heard the garage door open and they will be waiting for us and want to know what we have brought home. They also have their way of letting us know when it is time for them to get their night time treat and go to bed. If a stranger comes to the house, they hide until the coast is clear. I think their behavior and ours is pretty typical between pets and their owners.

This relationship which I have described between pets and their owners is also a good reference point as we talk about sheep and the good shepherd. Jesus makes a point of distinguishing between a good shepherd and the hireling that is just doing a job and has no real relationship with the sheep. What Jesus is describing as he talks about the good shepherd is a shepherd who has a relationship with the sheep. He cares about the sheep and provides for them, and they know the voice of their shepherd. This relationship is important as we approach the image of the good shepherd and Psalm 23 which also uses the images of shepherd and sheep. The context for both pictures is a relationship.

As Jesus asserts, "I Am the Good Shepherd," he is setting out the contours of his relationship with those who will follow him. Jesus says in verse 11 of John, "the good shepherd lays down his life for the sheep". There is a double sense here where Jesus is saying that he will protect the sheep at the risk of his own life. As Jesus repeats the promise to lay down his life a second time in verse 15 and a third time in verse 17, it is clear that his laying down of his life is more than a promise of protection. It is a fact, based on what he will do and the power and authority he has to do this on behalf of the sheep. Jesus makes it clear that he is laying down his life for the sheep in response to the Father's command and Jesus' love for the sheep. Jesus' laying down his life is an act of redemption for the benefit of the sheep. In the imagery of sacrifice, it is the shepherd who becomes the lamb of sacrifice. The depiction of Jesus as the triumphant lamb of the sacrifice is commonly shown with a sheep with a halo with a cross banner at its side in early Christian art. In verse 18, Jesus affirms that he is laying down his life for the fourth time noting that it is a willing act based on the need of the sheep. It is not an act where his life is taken by an enemy of the sheep. The reference, of course, is to the cross where Jesus will lay down his life. Jesus' action upon the cross, Jesus repeatedly tells us, is an act of giving that he does willingly. The laying down of his life is for the purpose of saving the sheep.

As Jesus further describes himself as the good shepherd, and the description is in terms of caring for the sheep. He has come that they might have life and have life to the full. The good shepherd's relationship with the sheep is rooted in love. Out of love, the good shepherd knows the sheep, and the sheep know him. The relationship between the good shepherd and the sheep is personal.

That sense of a personal relationship with the good shepherd was widely spread in the early church. This depiction of Jesus as the good shepherd was a common catacomb painting in the area around Rome. It was also a common motif carved into sarcophaguses of Christians in the second and third centuries. The sheep image is prominent in the apse semi-dome at the church of Santa Maria in Trastevere in Rome which is traditionally considered to be the first church opened for Christian worship in Rome. The sheep and shepherd image is also prominent in the apse semi-dome of San Clemente in Rome in a twelfth century mosaic. The image of Jesus as the good shepherd is not as prevalent in the late medieval period or in the art of the Renaissance. From an art perspective, the image of Jesus as the good shepherd makes a significant appearance again in the art of the eighteenth through twentieth century. It is a common church stain-glass depiction in that period in America.

The shepherd knows the sheep and the sheep know the shepherd. This knowledge leads to obedience. The sheep listen to the voice of the good shepherd. The same relationship of knowing is marked in the relationship between Jesus and the Father. Jesus models the behavior of listening as he listens to the Father and obeys his commands. The language of the 23rd Psalm also describes Jesus' relationship to the Father.

As we are talking about shepherds and sheep, we need to note that this is a descriptive image that the Old Testament uses to refer to God, the Father, and Israel. An early reference is Genesis 49:24 where the Father is named as "the Shepherd, the Rock of Israel." The prophet Jeremiah in Jeremiah 31:10 says, the Lord "will watch over his flock like a shepherd." Psalm 78:52-53 also picks up the image of God as a shepherd who has brought his flock out of Egypt.

But the classic image in the Old Testament which describes God as a shepherd is found in Psalm 23. As we take a look at this Psalm, we note again that the focus of the image is upon the relationship between the shepherd and the believer who is described in terms of a sheep.

David, in his song of faith, begins with "The Lord is my shepherd, I shall not want." David describes the relationship between the Lord and himself in personal terms from the beginning. The relationship is personal in the same way that the relationship between a shepherd and his sheep is personal. David describes the relationship in four sharp "He and me" pictures. He makes me. He leads me. He restores my soul. He guides me.

Jesus uses the same four sharp pictures as the shepherd who calls the sheep by name, leads them out, lays down his life for the sheep, and goes ahead of the sheep. The purpose of Jesus' laying down his life for the sheep was to restore their souls. The "He and me" pictures as used by David and as they are enlarged upon by Jesus' focus on the provision that shepherd makes for the sheep. Both illustrate the love and caring of the shepherd for the sheep. These images confirm why the shepherd is a good shepherd.

The 23rd Psalm moves beyond the "He and me" description of the relationship of the shepherd to the sheep by picturing a crisis situation for the sheep. "Even though I walk through the valley of the shadow of death" states the most severe crisis the sheep or the believer will face. Fear would be the expected reaction when traveling through the valley of the shadow of death. It is at this point that David brings back the shepherd image who takes away the fear of evil. The shepherd is there to protect the sheep in the valley of the shadow of death.

Jesus expands upon the reason that the sheep have no need of fear in the valley of the shadow of death. Four times in the "I Am the Good Shepherd" passage in the gospel of John, Jesus emphasizes laying down his life for the sheep. Jesus is developing not only a picture of protection from evil, but deliverance from evil. That deliverance from evil is what Jesus accomplished upon the cross. In that same context of deliverance from evil David says, "Your rod and staff they comfort me." The wood of the rod and staff remind me of the wood of the cross, the upright and the cross bar. Certainly, the Christian finds comfort in the cross knowing the love of God is demonstrated as Jesus lays down his life for us. The cross also points to Jesus entering the valley of the shadow of death ahead of the sheep, or follower. Jesus entered the valley of the shadow for the purpose of defeating death. Because of the resurrection of Jesus, believers enter the valley of the shadow of death not alone. Jesus has gone before us.

There is a change in the voice of the 23rd Psalm after the valley of the shadow from the "He" to the "You" voice. There follows two "you" pictures. You prepare and you anoint. It seems to me that these "you" pictures come across with a more intimate connection which also transcends the image of shepherd and sheep.

This is particularly true in the one picture of the 23rd Psalm that seems almost out of place with the imagery of a shepherd and sheep. "You prepare a table before me in the presence of my enemies." This picture does take on meaning in the context of Jesus as the Good Shepherd who prepares a table with bread and wine as symbols of his body broken and blood shed for the sheep. The bread and wine are symbols of Jesus laying down his life for the sheep. Jesus is the preparer of the table upon which He offers the food that brings life, relationship, and forgiveness. Judas, the betrayer, sat at that table, but none the less, the table was prepared and offered for all of the sheep. Judas is not only the betrayer of Jesus, but Judas also betrays the other eleven disciples, even as he offers a kiss in betrayal.

The next image "You anoint my head with oil" certainly speaks of the shepherd and sheep relationship as the shepherd used oil as a healing ointment for the wounds of the sheep. In the context of the New Testament, the same picture evokes the image of the anointing of oil that was offered with prayer in the name of the Lord for the healing of a believer (James 5:14).

The next image of "my cup overflows" certainly is suggestive of the overflowing of the spirit that was manifest on the day of Pentecost. The image is also suggestive of Jesus with the woman at the well as Jesus says, "The water I will give him will become in him a spring of water welling up to eternal life (John 4:14). Jesus expands upon the image in the Good Shepherd passage by saying, "I have come that they may have life, and have it to the full." In other translations the last phrase appears as "have it abundantly" (John 10:10).

The 23rd Psalm concludes with "surely goodness and mercy will follow me and I will dwell in the house of the Lord forever". The picture is an intimate picture that suggests the love of the Shepherd for the sheep which is eternal. Again, the concluding stanza is in harmony with the picture that Jesus draws of himself as the Good Shepherd who lays down his life and picks it up again so that the sheep may dwell with him in the Father's house.

Both the 23rd Psalm and the Good Shepherd passages from the gospel of John are about the relationship of God to the believer. We must note that for a relationship to truly exist there must be a response. The action cannot be all on one side if a there is to be a relationship. The response is implied in the 23rd Psalm and comes more from the sense of the proclamation David makes that the Lord is my shepherd, thus claiming the relationship. In the Good Shepherd picture that Jesus draws, the necessary response is more sharply drawn. Four times in this short passage Jesus notes that the sheep know and listen to the shepherd's voice. Knowing and listening to the voice is the mark of the sheep of the shepherd. Also implied is that the sheep which listen to the shepherd will follow the shepherd as he leads them.

The voice of the Good Shepherd is heard most clearly through the scriptures and through the Holy Spirit. There is implied a necessary getting acquainted and knowing of the shepherd even as the shepherd knows the sheep. The shepherd makes his presence known. It is left to the sheep to pay attention, listen, and to be discerning because there will be other voices that will lead the sheep astray. Discerning the voice of the shepherd in the midst of the babble in our world today is difficult, but it is critical to the well-being of the sheep.

David's proclamation that "The Lord is My Shepherd" is invitational. The psalm invites others to make the Lord their shepherd as well and to experience the love and grace of the shepherd. Jesus' proclamation "I Am the Good Shepherd" is also invitational. It invites others to listen for the voice of the shepherd. Those who hear the shepherd's voice are invited to be the sheep of the shepherd and follow him so that goodness and mercy will follow them and they will dwell in the house of the Lord forever.

Lesson Plan for Study

Get acquainted – How does your pet respond to you?

I. **The Lord is my Shepherd - Psalm 23**

    A. What attracts your attention in this passage of scripture?

    B. What does the shepherd do?

    C. What do the sheep do?

    D. How does the change from "he" to "you" strike you?

    E. Which image of shepherd resonates most with you?

II. **I Am the Good Shepherd – John 10: 11 - 18**

    A. What attracts your attention in the story?

    B. What does the shepherd do?

    C. What do the sheep do?

    D. What defines the shepherd as "good"?

    E. Who are the other sheep of a different sheep pen?

    F. How will the other sheep be known?

    G. Which image of Jesus as the good shepherd resonates most with you?

III. **How do the 23rd Psalm and the "I Am the Good Shepherd" passage interpret each other?**

    A. What does the 23rd Psalm add to the understanding of the good shepherd?

    B. How does Jesus as the good shepherd add to the 23rd Psalm?

    C. What do you learn about God from these two scriptures?

D. How does Jesus' use of "I Am" connect with the "I Am" of God?

E. How does the prepared table connect with Jesus as the preparer of the table?

F. How does the anointed head and overflowing cup relate to Jesus and the New Testament?

G. What is the most reassuring element of this image of the Shepherd as "I AM"?

LESSON 12

MANNA FROM HEAVEN AND I AM THE BREAD OF LIFE

Scripture

Manna from Heaven – Exodus 16:1-8
I Am the Bread of Life – John 6: 25 – 59

Context

The context for chapters eleven and twelve are the "I Am" statements of Jesus as recorded in the Gospel of John. The "I Am" statements also relate to the holy name of God as it was given to Moses at the burning bush, "I Am who I Am." Moses was to tell the Israelites, "I Am has sent me to you" (Exodus 3:14). John, as he records the seven "I Am" statements in his gospel, does so with the clear purpose of illustrating "that Jesus is the Messiah, the Son of God, and through believing you may have life in his name" (John 20:31). Each of the "I Am" statements builds off of images of God that were well established in the Old Testament.

The seven "I Am" statements in John were listed in chapter eleven. It is important to repeat here that the "I Am" statements are invitational in nature, inviting the believer into a relationship with Jesus. That invitation is so personal in the "I Am the Bread of Life" statement of Jesus in the gospel of John that it causes a sharp argument among his listeners. In verse 6:51, Jesus says, "I am the living bread that came down from heaven. If anyone eats of this bread, he will live forever. This bread is my flesh, which I will give for the life of the world."

In John 6, it is the crowd that initially raises the parallel to this "I Am" statement. They cite Moses and the manna in the wilderness. Jesus immediately develops this story about the exodus from Egypt as the pattern for Jesus' proclamation here and now that he is the Bread of life come down from heaven from the Father. This is the parallel that we will explore in chapter twelve. I believe it will be abundantly clear through the discussion that not only is this pair of scriptures an excellent example of the parallel pattern that we see in the Old and New Testament, but also all of the "I Am" statements will be reflected in the Old Testament as well.

Overview

Bread comes in many varieties: white bread, wheat, whole grain, rye, pumpernickel, rice, oat, corn, barley, hemp, and manna. Bread also comes in many forms: loaf bread, French bread, Italian bread, bagel, baguette, English muffin, pita, flatbread, rolls, buns, and pretzel bread. Bread comes in many types: leavened, unleavened, sourdough, and fruit bread. Bread is one of the oldest prepared foods in the history of the world. The builders of the pyramids were fueled by bread. This staple of every civilization upon the earth also has social implications. To share bread with a visitor is a sign of hospitality in many places. Many restaurants bring rolls to the table as the first food presented to a guest. To talk about bread is to talk about life.

Bread is the context for our parallel between the Old Testament and the New Testament in this chapter. The Old Testament passage comes from Exodus 16. The children of Israel have just left Egypt after 400 years of slavery in that land. Forty five days before the events of Exodus 16, the people of Israel had crossed the Red sea on dry land, and they watched as the waters closed back over the sea bed trapping the army of Pharaoh. They were freed by the mighty hand of God. They had witnessed ten plagues in Egypt, the dividing of the Red Sea, and the purification of the waters of Mara.

Now they were in the Desert of Sin, and the grumbling which had started earlier gets louder and is focused upon Moses and Aaron and by extension upon God. They complained that Moses and Aaron had brought them away from the abundant food of Egypt to starve in the desert. The complaint is an obvious exaggeration. God responds to the complaint saying he "will rain down bread from heaven for you." But, there are strings attached. God will use the bread from heaven, manna, as a teaching moment for Israel.

There are several lessons that God wants Israel to learn through the bread which comes down from heaven. First, He wants Israel to know who the source of all their provisions really is, namely Almighty God. Second, He desires to teach them obedience. They are to follow God's directions as He lays them out. Failure to follow the directions will result in spoiled food and hunger. Third, God wants them to learn to depend upon Him. Fourth, He wants them to note the special place of the Sabbath day. God will reinforce that teaching with the fourth commandment when they get to Mount Sinai. Fifth, the purpose of bread from heaven was so that Israel would know the Lord was their God. Israel would see the glory of God. Finally, God makes a promise for those who are obedient and depend upon God for their needs. He will provide bread from heaven until they safely arrive at the Promised Land. Bread from heaven will sustain Israel for the next forty years. The focus is on the bread from heaven which comes in the morning. But that was not the limit of God's provision. Quail descended upon the camp at night.

Manna, bread from heaven, will be placed in a pottery jar and will be kept as a testimony of God's provision (Exodus 16:32). That emphasis on the manna as a testimony is repeated three times in three verses. Manna will be yet another sign of the power of God and of his action on behalf of his people.

The New Testament parallel to this Old Testament pattern is found in John 6. Jesus has gone to the far side of the Sea of Galilee to a mountain side wilderness away from any town. A great crowd has gathered to hear Jesus teach. The scripture reminds us that the time of the Jewish Passover is near. The crowd is out on the mountain side for an extended period of time. The crowd is hungry. Jesus then takes the gift from a young boy and multiplies the 5 barley loaves and two fish into enough food to feed the whole crowd of over five thousand. The bread will become the focus, but fish was multiplied as well. The crowd responds to the miracle with an attempt to make Jesus king. Jesus, however, withdrew up into the mountain.

That night Jesus walks on the water of the sea and rejoins the disciples near Capernaum. The crowd catches up with Jesus at Capernaum and begins with a grumbling complaint. Through the discussion Jesus has with the crowd, the grumbling complaints will grow more serious as Jesus tries to direct them away from their search for signs and to open their eyes and believe in the one God has sent. The crowd, still focused on bread, brings up Moses and the manna in the wilderness. That is when Jesus says, "I Am the Bread of Life." The grumbling and complaints grow so strong that some turn away from Jesus and follow Him no more. Jesus then challenges the twelve disciples about whether they want to leave as well. It is then that Peter says, "Lord, you have the words of eternal life. We believe and know that you are the Holy One of God."

We have had a quick summary of the two stories. What will be helpful is to look at both stories together within the framework that is common to both stories. That framework includes the setting of the story, the grumbling and complaining of the people, the bread coming down from heaven, the invitation, the promise, and the testimony.

The settings of both stories have some striking similarities. Both are set near the Passover. There is also indirect pointing to another Passover where Jesus will share his Last Supper with the disciples. Both also show a crossing of water without getting wet. Israel crossed the Red Sea on dry Land. Jesus walked on the water across the Sea of Galilee. Both stories involve a confrontation with a large crowd of the people of Israel complaining against God. These shared settings reflect upon God's covenant with Israel. He is "the God of Abraham, Isaac, and Jacob," "I Am who I Am." It is he who sets the prisoner free, brings Israel out of slavery in Egypt, and will set his people free from their slavery to death. They also demonstrate God's love and patience with a people who are slow to understand and are persistent in their self-centered focus.

The grumbling and complaining that marks both stories is, on one hand, hard to understand. Israel has just escaped from Egypt. They have witnessed sign after sign that it was by the hand God that they had been set free. God has acted, and evidence of God's action was all around them. Yet, here they are forty five days from Egypt grumbling and complaining as if God was not the one who had saved them and was almighty in his power. The crowd seems to have no consciousness of God's presence. They assume that they are out in the wilderness alone with Moses and Aaron who are the focus of their anger.

Jesus' encounter with the grumbling crowd reveals their real interest in following Jesus. The crowd claims they want signs, but it is obvious that they, like Israel, will never get enough signs. It is a failure of belief. It is a failure to be God focused instead of self-focused. Grumbling and complaining is a warning sign to the believer; whether they are the children of Israel or the followers of Jesus. Grumbling signals a focus upon self instead upon God and his purposes.

Jesus presses the challenge to the crowd who seeks him out on the day after his multiplying the bread by proclaiming, "I Am the Bread of Life." It is a clear messianic claim. Immediately, it is challenged. The grumblers ask, "Is this not the son of Joseph?" They too seem to have no consciousness of being in the presence of God. Jesus is simply a miracle worker that they might use for their benefit. That lack of God consciousness extends to their reflection upon the bread in the wilderness which the crowd credits to Moses instead of to God.

Jesus quickly corrects them. It was not Moses who gave the children of Israel bread in the wilderness, but it was God who sent bread down from heaven. The bread was a sign of God being at work. Jesus then points them to God's presence in the present moment as he proclaims, "I am the living bread that comes down from heaven" (John 6:51). Jesus is saying that God, the Father, is at work in him, having sent Jesus from heaven. Jesus, as God's bread sent from heaven, is even more potent than the bread given to Israel in the wilderness. Jesus reminds the crowd that the children ate the bread come down from heaven in the wilderness, but they still died. Jesus, however, as the Bread of Life come down from heaven will give eternal life. They who eat of this living bread, which is his flesh, will live forever (John 6:51).

The crowd is unwilling to acknowledge that God was at work in their presence. They are offended by this claim of Jesus and will depart from him. Jesus acknowledges that their problem is one of belief - belief that God was at work in Jesus. Theirs is a failure to see that God was present and at work before their very eyes. It is the same failure as the children of Israel in the wilderness.

The command of God to Israel is to gather the manna on a daily basis except on the Sabbath, as a reminder of Israel's daily dependence upon God. Jesus taught the disciples to pray to God for daily bread. The theme of bread is accompanied in both stories by God's provision of sustaining meat. Quail fall upon the camp of Israel every evening around supper time. Jesus multiplies not only the bread of the boy's lunch but also the fish.

The theme of bread in Exodus is two-fold. The bread of the exodus is unleavened bread which was to be a memorial and testimony of God's deliverance from Egypt. It is also the manna gathered in the morning in the wilderness sent from heaven to sustain them on their journey to the Promised Land through the wilderness. God is specific in his instructions to Moses that this bread was also a testimony that was to be kept as a testimony of God at work in their lives.

The theme of bread in the gospel of John is also two-fold. It is the bread sent from heaven, namely Jesus Christ who is the Bread of Life. It is also the unleavened bread which is a part of Jesus' Last Supper with his disciples. The Last Supper was also a Passover meal. It is clear that Jesus is referring to the bread of the Last Supper yet to come in John 6:51. If you missed the point, Jesus states it even more clearly in John 6:53-58. When John recounts what happened in The Upper Room in chapters thirteen through seventeen, he does not refer directly to the broken bread and the cup which the disciples are to eat and drink. That sacramental reference in the Gospel of John is right here in John 6 as he speaks of the bread come down from heaven which is given for those who believe and will bring life to those who will eat and drink.

Jesus wants to be clear. It is God at work in him that will bring life to those who will open up their eyes to the presence of God and believe. Peter then sums up the desired response in John 6:68-69. "Lord, to whom can we go? You have the words of eternal life. We have come to believe and know that you are the Holy One of God." As Jesus, in the Upper Room, commands the disciples to remember him every time they eat the bread and drink the cup, it is clear that this action is to be an on-going activity of the followers of Jesus until they come to the Promised Land of heaven itself.

What Jesus was doing through his confrontation with the crowd at Capernaum was to invite them into a deeper relationship with God and himself. He wanted them to recognize the presence of God with them, and Jesus invites them to make the one who God has sent from heaven essential to their lives and to abide in him. It is the invitation to believe. As we have seen, Peter and the disciples affirm their decision to believe. Those who turned away are acknowledging their refusal of the invitation.

We see the same kind of invitation with Israel in the wilderness. The invitation takes the form of obedience. Will Israel follow instructions and live, or will they persist in following in their own way and die. The Lord has proclaimed, "I am your God." That is an invitation to respond by saying the Lord is my God, and I will follow Him in obedience.

The invitation, in both cases, has an element of testing. Will or will not the people follow through? Will they in fact make God the Lord of their life and eat of the provision He has made for them? The invitation becomes known in their hearts that the Lord He is God and opens their eyes to see the glory of the Lord. That theme courses through both stories.

The invitation, in both cases, comes with a promise. The promise of God in the wilderness is his continued presence that will sustain them all the way to the Promised Land which he will give to them. It is the promise of freedom from slavery, and the promise of life for Israel. The promise of Jesus, the Bread of Life, is that he gives himself so that those who believe will be sustained to eternal life. His promise is to abide in them.

The promise is sealed by a testimony in both cases. The testimony is a way of remembering that God has been at work. Moses, under the instructions of the Lord, tells Aaron to seal an omer of manna in a jar to place before the Lord as a covenant between God and Israel. The testimony is a reminder of God's provision and his action on behalf of Israel. It also serves as a reminder to Israel to be obedient to the word of God.

The testimony that Jesus outlines is clearly the Lord's Supper which is eaten and drank as a reminder that God is at work in the believer's life. Jesus is clear that participation in this testimony gives life to those who eat and drink. Jesus proclaims this is an action of God who has sent him from heaven for this purpose of bringing life. The believer receives the promise in their faithfulness to abide in Christ.

Both Jesus and the crowd of persons who joined him on the mountain side and ate bread and fish recognized that the provision of manna in the wilderness was a pattern for what was happening now in the presence of Jesus.

The song that strikes me as capturing the heart of both of these passages of scriptures is the hymn by John Sammis, "Trust and Obey". The first stanza goes: "When we walk with the Lord in the light of his word, what a glory he sheds on our way! While we do his good will, he abides with us still, and with all who will trust and obey. Trust and obey, for there's no other way to be happy in Jesus, but to trust and obey." That is the challenge presented by both stories. Trust and obey the Lord who is the source of life for you!

Lesson Plan for Study

Get acquainted – What is your favorite bread?

I. **Manna in the Wilderness – Exodus 16:1-8**

    A. What attracts your attention in this passage of scripture?
    B. What is hard to believe in the story?
    C. What is the purpose of God in sending bread from heaven?
    D. How does the Sabbath exemption strike you?
    E. What is the effect of the promise of God?

II. **I Am the Bread of Life – John 6:25 - 56**

    A. What attracts your attention in the story?
    B. What is hard to believe in the story?
    C. What is the purpose of God in sending bread from heaven?
    D. How does the imagery of the Last Supper strike you?
    E. What is the invitation of Jesus?
    F. What is the promise you hear in this passage?

III. **How do manna in the Wilderness and the "I Am the Bread of Life" passage interpret each other?**

    A. What does the manna in the wilderness add to the understanding of Jesus as the Bread of Life?
    B. How does Jesus, as the Bread of Life, add to the manna in the wilderness?
    C. What do you learn about God from these two scriptures?
    D. How does Jesus' use of "I Am" connect with the "I Am" of God?

E. How does the testimony of manna connect with the testimony of the Last Supper that Jesus instituted at the Passover meal with His disciples?

F. What does grumbling tell you about your relationship with God?

G. What is the most reassuring element of this image of Jesus as the Bread of Life?

CONCLUSION

One of the gifts that my wife and I received at our wedding was a painting of Cleopas and his companion walking with Jesus on the Emmaus road. I have always felt that Cleopas' companion was in fact his wife. The two of them invited the stranger who was explaining the scripture to them to come into their home and have supper with them. It was during the breaking of the bread at supper that they finally recognized Jesus for who He was. The Emmaus Road painting has inspired us. Cleopas and his companion said to each other, "Were not our hearts burning within us while he was talking to us on the road, while he opened the scriptures to us? (Luke 24:32)" The cause of their burning hearts was that Jesus had opened what we call the Old Testament and explained all the connections between Moses and the prophets and himself. I see Cleopas and his companion in the Upper Room during those ten days after the ascension of Jesus as they shared with the disciples all that Jesus had taught them. After the coming of the Holy Spirit, the burning hearts continued and the plan of God unfolded as the disciples studied the scriptures.

There have been many times during the writing of this book which explores these connections between the Old and New Testaments that my heart has burned within me as well. These connections give us a deeper appreciation of the scope of God's plan, the intensity and duration of God's love for us, and the constancy of his reaching out to connect with us.

I do not believe that I have come anywhere near exhausting the extent of these parallels between the Old and New Testaments. I would suggest a few more for your exploration. I have written about only 2 of the 7 "I Am" statements of Jesus, but I believe a case could be made for all 7 being parallels. There are some broad scope parallels such as the book of Revelation to the Old Testament prophets Ezekiel and Daniel. The book of Proverbs and the book of James also parallel each other in the assumption that faith is demonstrated by something you do.

Here are a few other parallels with a more narrow scope for exploration:

Crossing the Red Sea leading to 40 years in the Wilderness and The Baptism of Jesus and 40 days of Jesus in the Wilderness – Exodus 14-24 and Matthew 3:13-4:11

The Tabernacle in the Wilderness and the Cross of Christ
    Tabernacle – Exodus 25-27; Leviticus 16:1-34
    Cross of Christ – Matthew 27: 32-54, Hebrews 10

The Healing Ministry of Elijah and Elisha and the Healing Ministry of Jesus

David leading the procession of the Ark into Jerusalem and Jesus on Palm Sunday
    II Samuel 6:12-23, Luke 19:23-38

The suffering Servant of the Prophet Isaiah and Jesus

Life is in the Blood – Leviticus 17:11 and Ephesians 2:13

The Bronze Serpent in the Wilderness and Jesus on the Cross
    Numbers 21: 4-9; Luke 13: 33-49

Judah and Judas – Genesis 37: 25-36; Matthew 26:14, 47-56

There is one final parallel that highlights this critical connection between the Old Testament and the New Testament. This connection explores the shared understanding of the Word of God itself. These two parallels are Psalm 119: 1-2, 9, 45-46, 105 and II Timothy 3: 1-5, 14-17.

II Timothy has been called "the last will and testament" of the Apostle Paul written to his young friend from prison in Rome. Paul has already appeared before the Roman Governors Felix, Festus and King Agrippa while he was in Israel and made his defense for his actions by giving witness to his life and encounter with Jesus. Paul has "testified to the small and great alike ... saying nothing beyond what the prophets and Moses said would happen - that the Christ would suffer and be the first to rise from the dead, would proclaim light to his own people and to the Gentiles (Acts 26:22b-23)." We should note the correlation with Psalm 119:46 as the Psalmist speaks of declaring God's Word before kings.

After 2 years in prison in Caesarea, Paul appealed to the emperor in Rome, Nero. Appeals did not get expedited treatment in Rome. Paul spent at least 2 years in Rome under house arrest. But Paul didn't sit in jail feeling sorry for himself. He was busy proclaiming the gospel to everyone he encountered including the Praetorian Guard of the emperor. He wrote letters to the churches he established along with friends and the young pastors. Paul was busy.

Paul was also an eye witness to what was going on in the heart of the empire. He witnessed Nero proclaim himself a God. If Nero had been asked, he would have said that was the truth for him, and since he was the emperor, it was the truth for everyone. Paul heard the talk among the guards about the greed, the loss of self-control, the deceit and slander that went on everywhere. Rome was a place where good was called bad, and bad was called good, a place where truth was hard to find.

Paul knew what the problem was. The people of the Roman Empire did not know the one true God whom Jesus had come to make known. Paul knew what I saw on a sign at a car dealership a few months ago. "Without God anything is acceptable." When anything is acceptable, chaos will reign as people go from bad to worse, deceiving others and being deceived. Paul was witnessing the disintegration of the Roman Empire. The last verse of the book of Judges describes the chaos "as all the people did what was right in their own eyes." Paul knew there was only one way out of the problem. There is only one way that leads to life.

So Paul wrote to his young friend Timothy with the same advice that the Psalmist gives the young man who seeks his way in the 119th Psalm. We today need to listen up, because Paul's observations are on the mark with our society. The Psalmist says, "God's word is a lamp to our feet and a light to our path." Paul was in chains, as he reminds Timothy that the Word of God is not chained.

In a dark world where truth is ignored, where deceit and the half-truth are used to slander and mislead, where people are lovers of pleasure rather than lovers of God; a young man needs a light to guide his way. So do old men.

I do not like driving much in the dark anymore. It is hard to see in the dark. Too much remains hidden in the dark. My imagination works overtime in the dark. Our fears tend to come out in the dark. Crime clearly abounds in the dark. What we really need is light so that we can see.

Jesus knows our need and proclaims: "I am the Light of the world." With that proclamation Jesus healed the man who had been born blind. In the former blind man's interaction with the Pharisees in the 9th chapter of John it is clear that not only has the blind man's physical sight been restored, but he also has spiritual sight and recognizes God at work in his life. He has seen the truth and it makes him free.

So the apostle Paul wrote to his young friend in order to help Timothy find his way in such a world telling him, "but as for you, continue in what you have learned …how from childhood you have known the sacred writings that are able to instruct you for salvation through faith in Christ Jesus (II Timothy 3:14-15)."

Paul is saying, Timothy, the Word of God will bring light to your path. It is clear that such light is needed desperately today. The Bible, today, is under attack more than ever. Truth telling is harder to find than ever. The insistence that I can do whatever is right in my own eyes is seen everywhere, which also explains why the Bible is under attack today. Each person seeks to be an authority unto themselves.

The Apostle Paul began to explain to Timothy the power of the scriptures. First of all, Paul reminded Timothy of the origin of the scriptures. They are inspired by God; they are God breathed. The scripture is not of human origin. Oh, they are written by men, to be sure, but they are God's idea. They are His gift of light for our path.

Psalm 119 reminds us that God's word is firmly fixed in heaven (Psalm119:89). This is not just a transient word useful to a few people, but God's eternal word that illuminates truth that is firmly fixed. There is objective truth which is the only solid foundation for living. To miss that truth is to step out on quicksand. God's Word is not only life but a blessing to us (Psalm119:2) and delight (Psalm 119:77) better than gold and silver (Psalm 119:72).

Second, Paul said that scripture is useful for teaching. No one becomes a disciple of Jesus Christ by accident. It's a choice to follow Jesus. Neither do we grow in our faith by accident; that too is a choice, a choice to ground ourselves in God's word.

Grounding himself in God's Word was a choice that Jesus made. Matthew shows us Jesus in the wilderness being tempted. The temptation came in the devil's words, "If you are the Son of God, command these stones to become loaves of bread (Matthew 4:3)." Jesus answered from the scripture what he had internalized in his heart. "It is written, man shall not live by bread alone, but by every word that proceeds from the mouth of God (Deuteronomy 8:3)."

Jesus knew the scriptures as God breathed, useful for teaching. Would you like a resource to teach your children about what really matters in life? Would you like a resource that would teach you how life works best, an instruction manual straight from the manufacturer of this world? Knowledge is a powerful tool. We invest lots of money into all kinds of education. Ought we not to invest our time and resources into getting to know this book that can guide our path through life?

Third, Paul told Timothy the scripture is useful for reproof and correction. The number one lesson my father taught me in construction was measure twice, cut once. Re-check or re-proof your information before you act. There are times in that re-proof where we find we had made a mistake and need to correct the numbers we had written down.

One of the reasons some people reject the Bible today is that they do not want to be corrected. They will not take the time to reproof how they are living their lives because they want to do what they want to do!

Today there is a battle going on for our minds. Some people are swayed by what they see and hear on television, some by the latest blog postings, or others by the last conversation that they had. They hear one thing, so they go in that direction. Then they hear something else and go another direction. That kind of roving authority leads to a dangerous "if-it-feels-good-do-it" mind set. It also leaves us as the last authority on any issue.

One television commercial says, "A mind is a terrible thing to waste." That's true. God has given us wonderful minds, and he wants us to make the best use of them. He wants us to have the mind of Christ - to think like Jesus. The Bible is where we learn what God thinks and how God sees things. When we see things only from a human point of view, life can be comfortable. I am doing what I want to do. However, it can be uncomfortable to see things from God's point of view about what really matters.

I believe the number one temptation that keeps us from reading the Bible is that it is much easier to drift with the crowd than it is to share God's viewpoint and be at odds with the world.

Yet, if we are to have the mind of Christ, we must bring ourselves to scripture. The scriptures have the truth that can light our path to eternity.

Next, Paul tells Timothy the scriptures are useful in training for righteousness. Is righteousness the goal of your life? If not then wrong doing is most certainly the path you are on. Psalm 119 is constant in its portrayal of these two paths. The Word leads to life. Indifference or neglect of the Word leads to death.

Paul has a goal in mind. He wants to reflect the image of Jesus Christ. He wanted to reclaim the image in which God first created us. He wanted to have more in common with God. He wanted to stay in training as a member of God's team. Unfortunately surveys today suggest that 55% of Christians do not open their Bibles even once a week. No book is sold more and read less than the Bible. That doesn't sound like committed training.

Why do we need to spend time in God's Word? For the same reason the athlete needs to spend time training in the gym. We need to train our minds so that when the choices of life come rushing at us, we can do what we practiced in our minds because we have trained our minds to make the right choice. This is also the constant theme of Psalm119.

Training in the Word is what I think was happening when Cleopas and his companion were on their way to Emmaus on Easter Sunday evening when the stranger joined them on the road. The stranger took them through Moses and all the prophets explaining why the Messiah had to suffer and die. At Emmaus, the stranger was finally recognized as Jesus broke bread for them. The response of Cleopas and his companion was "Were not our hearts burning within us while he was talking to us on the road, while he was opening the scriptures to us (Luke 24:32)?" Have you experienced that burning of your heart as the scripture is opened to you? That is part of the joy of allowing the light to illuminate your way.

Finally, Paul reminded Timothy that there is a purpose for this training. The purpose is for every man and woman of God to be complete and equipped for every good work.

Over the years, I have accumulated a lot of tools. I want to be equipped. Trying to get a wrench to substitute for a hammer is a real bummer. If there is anything I hate, it is trying to do those handyman projects and not being properly equipped.

But that is what happens today in the matter of our faith. Instead of being properly equipped with the Word of God, we try to meet the challenges before us by using popular opinion instead of God's Word. Then, we wonder why we find ourselves in trouble as a result.

We need God's equipment for every good work. I believe most persons desire to make a difference for good in this world. I believe they want to impact their family and friends for good. We want this world to be a better place for our having been here. The power to do that comes as we live the Father's way. The Father's way is given to us in His Word!

John Wesley called himself a "man of one book," even though he was widely read. For John Wesley, the Bible was the central, indispensable resource for the Christian faith. He depended upon the word for guidance, comfort, and strength. John Wesley too felt the burning heart as the book of Romans was opened up for him at Aldersgate. Like Paul's desire for young Timothy, it instructed him for salvation through faith in Jesus Christ.

Salvation through faith in Jesus Christ is also my desire for each of you who read this book. God has a wondrous life planned for each one of us and that is why he sent his Son to die and rise from the dead for us. The complexity and the thousands of years that his plan spans give us a feel for the depth of his love. It is not a passing fancy. He has also given his Word that we might be equipped for his purpose. I pray that you heart burns within you every time you open His book!

Printed in the United States
By Bookmasters